Consumer Credit Costs, 1949–59

NATIONAL BUREAU OF ECONOMIC RESEARCH
STUDIES IN CONSUMER INSTALMENT FINANCING

CONSUMER CREDIT COSTS 1949–59

BY

PAUL F. SMITH

UNIVERSITY OF PENNSYLVANIA

A STUDY BY THE
NATIONAL BUREAU OF ECONOMIC RESEARCH

PUBLISHED BY
PRINCETON UNIVERSITY PRESS
PRINCETON, NEW JERSEY

1964

Printed in the United States of America

v

RELATION OF THE DIRECTORS TO THE WORK AND PUBLICATIONS OF THE NATIONAL BUREAU OF ECONOMIC RESEARCH

1. The object of the National Bureau of Economic Research is to ascertain and to present to the public important economic facts and their interpretation in a scientific and impartial manner. The Board of Directors is charged with the responsibility of ensuring that the work of the National Bureau is carried on in strict conformity with this object.

2. To this end the Board of Directors shall appoint one or more Directors of Research.

3. The Director or Directors of Research shall submit to the members of the Board, or to its Executive Committee, for their formal adoption, all specific proposals concerning researches to be instituted.

4. No report shall be published until the Director or Directors of Research shall have submitted to the Board a summary drawing attention to the character of the data and their utilization in the report, the nature and treatment of the problems involved, the main conclusions, and such other information as in their opinion would serve to determine the suitability of the report for publication in accordance with the principles of the National Bureau.

5. A copy of any manuscript proposed for publication shall also be submitted to each member of the Board. For each manuscript to be so submitted a special committee shall be appointed by the President, or at his designation by the Executive Director, consisting of three Directors selected as nearly as may be one from each general division of the Board. The names of the special manuscript committee shall be stated to each Director when the summary and report described in paragraph (4) are sent to him. It shall be the duty of each member of the committee to read the manuscript. If each member of the special committee signifies his approval within thirty days, the manuscript may be published. If each member of the special committee has not signified his approval within thirty days of the transmittal of the report and manuscript, the Director of Research shall then notify each member of the Board, requesting approval or disapproval of publication, and thirty additional days shall be granted for this purpose. The manuscript shall then not be published unless at least a majority of the entire Board and a two-thirds majority of those members of the Board who shall have voted on the proposal within the time fixed for the receipt of votes on the publication proposed shall have approved.

6. No manuscript may be published, though approved by each member of the special committee, until forty-five days have elapsed from the transmittal of the summary and report. The interval is allowed for the receipt of any memorandum of dissent or reservation, together with a brief statement of his reasons, that any member may wish to express; and such memorandum of dissent or reservation shall be published with the manuscript if he so desires. Publication does not, however, imply that each member of the Board has read the manuscript, or that either members of the Board in general, or of the special committee, have passed upon its validity in every detail.

7. A copy of this resolution shall, unless otherwise determined by the Board, be printed in each copy of every National Bureau book.

(Resolution adopted October 25, 1926,
as revised February 6, 1933, and February 24, 1941)

vi

Contents

Tables

Appendix Tables

Charts

Acknowledgments

I AM particularly indebted to John M. Chapman of Columbia University and to Geoffrey H. Moore and Robert P. Shay of the National Bureau staff for their help in planning the study and advice on the analysis and presentation of the results. Other members of the National Bureau staff who reviewed earlier drafts and made thoughtful suggestions are Reuben Kessel, Anna J. Schwartz, and F. Thomas Juster. Robert W. Johnson of Michigan State University contributed helpful comments. I am also indebted to members of the Advisory Committee of the Consumer Credit Study, listed in the Foreword, who aided in the planning of the investigation and offered critical comments on drafts of this report, and to the reading committee of the National Bureau's Board of Directors, Francis M. Boddy, Wallace J. Campbell, and A. J. Hayes.

Special acknowledgment is due the financial institutions which contributed data to the study. Particular mention should be made of the help given by William S. Germer and H. F. Wright, Jr., of the First Pennsylvania Bank and Trust Company, Ernst A. Dauer of Household Finance Corporation, M. R. Neifeld and Charles A. Loeffler of Beneficial Management Corporation, R. F. Murphy of General Motors Acceptance Corporation, and George F. Dimmler, formerly of C. I. T. Financial Corporation. Roland M. Gardner and other staff members of the Bureau of Federal Credit Unions advised on the use of the credit union data.

Statistical and accounting assistance was capably given by Florence Liang of the National Bureau and V. N. Vora of the University of Pennsylvania. Christine Culbert, of the National Bureau editorial staff, provided editorial assistance. H. Irving Forman drew the charts.

Foreword

PAUL F. SMITH's study represents an extension of the survey of financial structure and operating characteristics of consumer credit agencies and commercial banks in the National Bureau's earlier Studies in Consumer Instalment Financing. The tenth volume of that series, *Comparative Operating Experience of Consumer Instalment Financing Agencies and Commercial Banks, 1929–41* by Ernst A. Dauer, published in 1944, is the direct predecessor to this volume.

Smith explores the interrelations between rates of charge and major cost components of four major types of financial institutions: consumer finance companies, sales finance companies, commercial banks, and federal credit unions. These institutions extend a wide range of consumer credit in varying forms. His study presents comparative cost data for the eleven years, 1949 through 1959. An earlier report, dealing with 1959 alone, was published in the September 1962 issue of the *Journal of Finance* and reprinted as Occasional Paper 83 by the National Bureau under the title *Cost of Providing Consumer Credit: A Study of Four Major Types of Financial Institutions.* This work is part of a broad study of consumer credit, which is designed to assess its role in the functioning of the economy of the United States.

Since 1941 there have been striking changes in the holdings of consumer credit outstanding. When the Dauer study was completed, sales finance companies were the largest holders of consumer instalment credit outstanding, followed closely by commercial banks and retail outlets. By the end of 1959 commercial banks had become the predominant holders of consumer credit followed by sales finance companies and retail outlets. Credit unions showed marked gains during the intervening years. The striking growth of consumer credit stimulated widespread interest in the costs of providing credit among institutional sources. The difficulties of cost allocations and the lack of uniform cost accounting procedures have long delayed the acquisition of cost data for consumer credit operations among the major types of credit institutions. By working with small samples of companies with comparable cost accounting procedures, Smith has succeeded in isolating consumer credit costs and, in some cases, he supplies separate cost estimates by type of credit. Although the data cannot be considered representative of all institutions within each of the major types, they are certainly typical of many large credit suppliers within the finance company and bank groups, and they do cover all credit unions.

Special acknowledgment should be made to the Advisory Committee

xvii

of the Consumer Credit Study, which assisted in drafting plans for this investigation, conferred with staff and authors at several stages of the work, and reviewed the final manuscript. Individuals who served on this committee are: Paul W. McCracken, chairman, University of Michigan; Gordon E. Areen, Associates Investment Company; Frank Barsalou, Pacific Finance Corporation; Dorothy S. Brady, University of Pennsylvania; John M. Chapman, Columbia University; Mona Dingle, Division of Research and Statistics, Board of Governors of the Federal Reserve System; Bertrand Fox, Harvard University; Raymond W. Goldsmith, Yale University; Robert E. Lewis, First National City Bank of New York; Roger F. Murray, National Bureau of Economic Research; Roland I. Robinson, Michigan State University; Herbert Stein, Committee for Economic Development; Van Buren Thorne, Jr., General Motors Acceptance Corporation; and William L. Wilson, C. I. T. Financial Corporation. Others who formerly served on the advisory committee are George Dimmler, George W. Omacht, Sidney E. Rolfe, and LeRoy A. Weller.

The National Bureau also wishes to express its thanks to those organizations that cooperated in providing materials for this study:

Consumer Finance Companies
American Investment Company of Illinois
Beneficial Finance Company
Family Finance Corporation
Household Finance Corporation
Interstate Finance Corporation
Liberty Loan Corporation
Merchants Acceptance Corporation
Seaboard Finance Company
State Loan and Finance Corporation

Sales Finance Companies
American Discount Company
Associate Investment Company
C. I. T. Financial Corporation
General Acceptance Corporation
General Finance Corporation
General Motors Acceptance Corporation
Interstate Securities Company
Pacific Finance Corporation
Securities Acceptance Corporation
Southwestern Investment Company

Commercial Banks
Bankers Trust Company
Bank of America NT-SA
City National Bank & Trust Co.
First National Bank of Boston
First National City Bank of New York
First Pennsylvania Banking & Trust Co.
Marine Trust Company of Western New York
National Shawmut Bank
Pittsburgh National Bank
Provident Tradesmen's Bank & Trust
Security First National Bank
United California Bank
Valley National Bank
Wells Fargo Bank American Trust Company

Credit Unions
Bureau of Federal Credit Unions, U. S. Department of Health, Education, and Welfare

Other projects in the Consumer Credit Study are closely related to the material in this volume. An analysis of the rate structure in automobile financing by Robert P. Shay will provide detailed estimates of the cost to consumers of financing the purchase of new and used automobiles. Wallace P. Mors is investigating economic aspects of the regulatory policies of states toward consumer credit. The effects of credit use upon the management of consumer finances are being studied by F. Thomas Juster. Richard T. Selden is conducting an investigation of the flow of funds from their sources through financial markets to their ultimate use by consumers. Finally, the impact of consumer indebtedness upon unemployed families is being appraised by Philip A. Klein.

The Consumer Credit Study was made possible by research grants to the National Bureau from four finance companies: Associates Investment Company, C. I. T. Financial Corporation, General Motors Acceptance Corporation, and Pacific Finance Corporation. In addition, the Wharton School of Finance and Commerce of the University of Pennsylvania permitted use of the author's time and facilities made available through a chair in consumer credit given to the University by the Family Finance Corporation.

These institutions are, of course, not to be held responsible for any of the statements made or views expressed here.

Robert P. Shay
Director, Consumer Credit Study

Consumer Credit Costs, 1949–59

CHAPTER 1

Introduction and Summary

THE $63.5 billion of consumer credit outstanding at the end of 1962 was supplied by a wide variety of retail and financial institutions, ranging from small cooperatives to million-dollar financial organizations. It varied in form from small unsecured loans to long-term contracts of thousands of dollars protected by valuable collateral. Some of it was advanced directly to consumers and some of it was purchased from retailers in large-volume operations. As might be expected, the cost of providing this credit differed with the type of credit extended and with the conditions under which it was supplied.

The need for better information about the cost of granting consumer credit arises from many social and economic problems. Large differences in the finance charges paid by consumers for credit prompt questions about the reasons for such differences and, at times, about the "fairness" of the charges. Answers to economic questions about the growth and cyclical behavior of consumer credit depend on the extent of our knowledge of the cost of lending to consumers and the factors affecting these costs. An understanding of the consumer credit industry—its organization, structure, and forms of competition—requires knowledge about the nature of costs and the relationship of these costs to the size and institutional structure of the participants. The purpose of this study is to develop information that will give some insight into these questions.

The study is based on information from four major types of financial institutions engaged in extending credit to consumers: commercial banks, sales finance companies, consumer finance companies, and federal credit unions.[1] These institutions together held 70 per cent of all consumer credit and 90 per cent of all instalment credit outstanding at the end of 1959.[2] Commercial banks held the largest share of outstanding instalment credit—38 per cent; sales finance companies held 26 per cent; and consumer finance companies and credit unions each held slightly less than 10 per cent.

Data were obtained for nine commercial banks, ten sales finance companies, nine consumer finance companies, and all federal credit

---

[1] The study supplements and brings up to date an earlier study of consumer credit cost conducted by Ernst A. Dauer for the National Bureau and entitled *Comparative Operating Experience of Consumer Instalment Financing Agencies and Commercial Banks, 1929–41.*

[2] Outstanding instalment credit at the end of 1959, the last year covered by the study, amounted to $39 billion.

unions.[3] The agencies included held one-fifth of all instalment credit outstanding at the end of 1959 and one-fourth of the credit held by the type of institution they represented. Although the samples covered a relatively small number of companies, they accounted for more than half of the consumer credit in their segments of the industry, except the sample of commercial banks which held only 7 per cent of the consumer credit held by all banks. A description of the samples and of the processing of the data is presented in Appendix A.

The institutions covered by the study operated in very different legal and institutional environments. None of these companies engaged solely in lending to consumers. All of them made other types of loans, provided insurance, or engaged in other activities. In some cases, consumer credit was a relatively small part of their total business.

The integration of consumer credit with the other activities made it difficult to isolate the cost of consumer credit operations. The scope of the investigation was necessarily limited by the availability of accounting information and by the difficulties and perplexities of standardizing the information from various sources. In many cases, cost accounting records had to be used to separate the cost of consumer credit operations, and, in some cases, estimates of certain types of costs had to be prepared.

The word "cost" means many different things to different people. The lender views cost as the part of the finance charge that has to be used to cover expenses. The economist views cost as including "normal profit," which is defined as the return on capital that is essential to the retention of funds in the industry. In a competitive industry, extraordinary profits or less than normal profits exist only during the short run either for the individual company or the industry as a whole. Extraordinary profits attract new funds and less than normal profits lead to the withdrawal of funds. For purposes of this study, the lender's profit was regarded as an element of cost although profits are shown separately as well.

Companies that engage in providing joint services or products have some freedom in their pricing policies. As a result, the profits on any one type of joint activity, such as consumer credit, may be more or less than those required to produce a "normal" return on the company's net

---

[3] Credit unions that are chartered under state laws and are nearly as numerous as those under federal charter were not covered by the study because uniform data on costs were not obtainable.

worth. High earning on services sold with consumer credit, such as credit life insurance or insurance on the collateral, may permit the lender to offer lower rates on credit. In such cases, part of the cost of consumer credit (normal profit of the lender) may be absorbed by other activities. Or the opposite may be the case: part of cost of related activities may be absorbed in charges on consumer credit. The possibility of substitution of this type makes it necessary to examine the profits on consumer credit in conjunction with the over-all profits of the company.

Most of the tabulations in the study were developed from annual income and expense data and from end-of-year balance sheets. Averages of beginning- and end-of-year balance sheet data were used in all ratios of income and expense data to balance sheet data. Most of the ratios dealing with the cost of consumer credit are expressed in dollars per $100 of credit receivables while ratios reflecting the over-all operations of the companies are expressed in percentages.

Financial ratios for banks and finance companies were calculated from these statements for each company and simple arithmetic averages of all sample companies were computed to represent each type of financial institution. Thus, each company receives an equal weight in the average of financial ratios, regardless of its size. This system of weighting the sample companies as units instead of by dollar volume of credit was adopted to avoid domination of income and expense relationships by the largest firms in samples of nine or ten companies. Weighting each company equally, on the other hand, gives the smaller companies greater weight in the averages than is justified by their size. Since the finance company and bank samples were drawn primarily from large firms, the unit weighting was considered a better representation of the rate-cost relationships characteristic of the institutional framework. In certain instances, notably those dealing with average charges, alternative calculations are given with each company weighted by its receivables in order to illustrate differences attributable to the method of weighting.

Financial ratios for credit unions, on the other hand, were available only from aggregate data which give each credit union a weight according to the dollar amount of each item included. The differences involved in a comparison of credit union averages with those of other institutions with different unit weights are minimized by two considerations. First, the credit union sample is large and representative since it includes all federally chartered credit unions, and, second, variations in size among credit unions are less than among banks and finance companies.

3

Summary

Average finance charges on the consumer credit provided by the four types of institutions studied varied from $24 per $100 of credit outstanding for one type to $9 for another in 1959. Most of the variation in finance charges was attributable to differences in operating expenses, rather than to differences in nonoperating expenses including the lender's profits. The profits of the stockholder-owned institutions averaged 9.9 per cent of net worth, which was within the range of profits recorded by manufacturing corporations.

Among the four types of institutions, operating expenses, which ranged from $3.30 to $14.25 per $100 of outstanding credit, were found to vary directly with finance charges. Many factors contributed to the spread in costs. The method of acquiring business, whether obtained directly from the public or indirectly from dealers, caused variations in advertising and occupancy expenses. Differences in the character of risks were reflected in loss ratios ranging from 15 cents per $100 of outstanding credit at commercial banks to a figure eleven times as large at consumer finance companies. Variations in the size of credit contracts resulted in differences in the number of contracts that had to be handled for a given dollar volume of credit and in the cost per $100 of credit outstanding. It was estimated that in 1959 the sample consumer finance companies, which had the smallest average contract size, handled twenty-three contracts for each $10,000 of new business while commercial banks handled less than half that number. Legal provisions controlling operating practices and assistance provided by members and sponsors of credit unions added to cost differentials.

Smaller, but still significant, differences in the cost of providing consumer credit were traced to the methods of financing and to variations in income tax provisions. The four types of institutions obtained equity and nonequity funds from many different sources. The cost of nonequity funds ranged from 1.2 to 4.6 per cent. The effectiveness with which they were able to use resources and the extent to which they were able to obtain debt financing affected the cost of money used in providing credit to consumers.

The study revealed several trends in finance charges among the sample companies during the rapid growth of credit in the 1950's. First, the average finance charge at both types of finance company and federal credit unions declined during this period. Sales finance companies experienced the largest decline. Second, the average finance charge at commercial banks increased during the last five years of the 1950's, reflecting both an increase in rates by type of credit and an increase in the proportion of personal loans included in the average. A third trend, reflecting in part the first two, was a decrease in the spread in rates between the highest-cost and lowest-cost institutions.

These trends developed during a period when all segments of the industry were participating in a threefold expansion of outstanding instalment credit. The share of the total held by commercial banks and both types of finance companies showed little change, but the share of credit unions increased from 3.8 to 8.4 per cent of the total during the 1950's.

The sample finance companies and federal credit unions were able to reduce operating expenses per $100 of outstanding credit during the 1950's despite increases in wage rates and other prices. This reduction was possible in part because of an increase in the average contract size and in the accompanying decline in per dollar handling costs. In contrast, operating costs at commercial banks increased slightly during the last half of the decade, despite increasing contract size.

Only minor changes in the composition of costs were observed. Advertising costs decreased slightly at consumer finance companies but increased at sales finance companies and banks. Other operating costs varied with changes in total expenses.

The sharp rise in general interest rates during the 1950's added to the cost of nonequity funds used in instalment lending. The impact of this change was particularly strong at both types of finance company and resulted in a reduction in their profits. They were able to mitigate the effects of rising interest and other expenses on profits by increasing the proportion of debt to equity financing; by using resources more efficiently, i.e., by reducing the proportion of assets held in nonearning forms; and by improving their earnings from activities other than consumer credit.

The cost of nonequity funds increased at both commercial banks and credit unions as a result of higher interest rates. But the effects were much less important than in the case of finance companies. Commercial banks were affected by rising rates only as they paid more for time deposits. Nonequity funds were of minor importance to credit unions and they were more than able to absorb the increased cost of these funds by a reduction in the cost of their nonearning assets. At both commercial banks and federal credit unions, the increase in general interest rates provided a higher return on the nonconsumer assets which more than offset the effects of higher costs of funds on their over-all return.

CHAPTER 2
Consumer Finance Companies

CONSUMER finance companies engage primarily in making personal loans to consumers and are identified and defined by their operations under state small-loan laws. Although these laws differ in detail from state to state, they are similar in content and scope. They provide for the licensing and supervision of small-loan operations and specify many of the terms and conditions of the loans. Licensing requirements include proof of the character, fitness, and financial responsibility of the applicant and frequently call for evidence that the proposed office will result in "convenience and advantage" to the community. The regulatory provisions of these laws set maximum rates of charge, usually scaled downward as the size of the loan increases; regulate fees; establish ceilings on loan size; and frequently specify the methods that can be used in computing finance charges and many of the operating details of extending and collecting credit.

Consumer finance companies held $3.3 billion in consumer loans at the end of 1959. They ranged from large nationwide companies with hundreds of millions of dollars in loans to single-office operations with only a few thousand dollars in loans. This study covers nine large companies that were willing and able to provide the detailed cost data. They do not necessarily represent all segments of the industry. The companies included, however, held 70 per cent of the loans of all consumer finance companies at the end of 1959 and represented a sizable segment of the industry. The sample is described in greater detail in Appendix A.

Extent of Specialization

Although consumer finance companies operate primarily under state small-loan laws, most of them have diversified their operations to some extent, and nearly all of them now provide credit life insurance, purchase sales finance paper, or make additional loans under other state laws. Some of these activities may be handled by a subsidiary or by the parent or operating company. All of the companies covered by the study engaged in some activities other than lending under small-loan laws. Most of them made other types of loans or purchased automobile or appliance paper. They all provided credit life insurance for their borrowers.

The companies included in the study invested 87 per cent of their assets in consumer credit receivables in 1959 and 1 per cent in other earning assets of all types (Table 1). The proportion of consumer lend-

6

TABLE 1

USES OF FUNDS BY CONSUMER FINANCE COMPANIES, END OF 1959
(per cent)

Item	Mean Distribution	Range of Ratios[a] Maximum	Minimum
Earning assets, net	87.7	94.6	82.0
Consumer credit	86.5	94.4	80.0
Automobile paper	1.8	15.7	0
Other consumer goods paper	6.8	21.5	0
Personal loans	77.9	94.3	53.7
Other	1.2	5.8	0
Cash and bank balances	9.0	14.6	2.7
Other assets	3.3	4.5	2.2
Total	100.0	--	--

Source: Nine-company sample.

[a]Components in columns for maximum and minimum ratios are not additive as ratios for individual items were taken from statements of different companies.

ing varied slightly from company to company, but in all cases dominated their lending activities. The company most engaged in other activities had only 6 per cent of its funds invested in nonconsumer credit or in other earning assets at the end of 1959.

Consumer credit receivables of the companies surveyed were highly concentrated in personal loans. Such loans on an average accounted for 78 per cent of total assets and nine-tenths of their consumer receivables in 1959. However, one company reported only 54 per cent of its assets and three-fourths of its consumer receivables in personal loans.

Gross Finance Charges

Gross finance charges averaged $24.04 per $100 of outstanding credit at the nine sample companies in 1959.[1] At individual companies, average charges ranged from a high of $31.58 to a low of $20.02. Nearly all of this amount was received by the consumer finance company in the form of finance charges or fees. A small amount, estimated at 17 cents per

[1] Weighted averages based on the dollar amount of loans outstanding at each company show slightly different levels and changes (see Table 35).

7

$100, was credited to retailers under dealer participation agreements in connection with purchases of instalment contracts.

Although these charges cover all types of consumer credit held by these companies, they do not differ greatly from the average for personal loans. Gross finance charges on personal loans at consumer finance companies averaged $24.89 per $100, or less than a dollar higher than the average for loans of all types. Charges on other types of loans were not computed separately because the outstanding amount of such loans varied so widely over time that reliable rates could not be computed from averages of year-end figures.

Finance charges at consumer finance companies declined steadily during the eleven years covered by the study (Chart 1). From 1949 to 1959, the average charge decreased by $2.03 per $100, or 8 per cent. This decline followed a longer-run trend that began in the midthirties. The gross finance charges at the two largest companies, as measured by the ratio of total earnings to average receivables, declined from $35 per $100 in 1933 to $30 in 1941 and to $21.74 by 1959.[2] Data for another group of companies show a similar trend, but completely comparable data are not available for an accurate comparison.

The increase in the average size of loan probably played a major role in the decline in finance charges at these companies. The increase was 2.7 times from 1939 to the end of 1959 and 70 per cent between 1949 and 1959.[3] This expansion in loan size reflected both an increase in legal ceilings and the demands of borrowers. The larger loan size permitted a reduction in the per dollar handling costs and, in states with graduated rates, resulted in changes in the applicable legal maxima. Since graduated rate ceilings are scaled downward as the size of the loan increases, an increase in the average size of a loan reduces the average maximum charge. Although the scale of rates varies from state to state and was altered by numerous legislative changes during the period covered, the following example for the State of Colorado indi-

[2] The ratio of total income to average consumer credit receivables is not as accurate a measure as the more refined ratio of consumer credit income to consumer credit receivables used for recent periods. The difference in these ratios was small for the two largest companies, however. The average ratio of total earnings to consumer credit receivables for these companies in 1959 was $21.74 per $100 compared with the ratio of consumer credit income to consumer credit receivables of $21.62 per $100. Data for the period before 1949 were obtained from Ernst A. Dauer, *Comparative Operating Experience of Consumer Instalment Financing Agencies and Commercial Banks, 1929-41,* New York, NBER, 1944, p. 84.

[3] *The Consumer Finance Industry,* National Consumer Finance Association, Englewood Cliffs, 1962, Table 4-3, p. 59.

CHART 1
Gross Finance Charges on Consumer Credit at Consumer Finance Companies, 1930–41 and 1949–59
(per $100 of average outstanding credit)

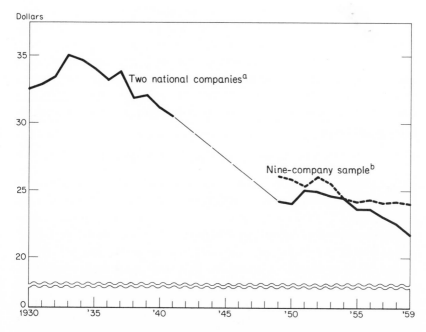

Source: Data for two national companies for 1930–41 obtained from Dauer, *Comparative Operating Experience of Consumer Instalment Financing Agencies and Commercial Banks, 1929–41*. Data for 1949–59 from information collected from sample of nine companies are reproduced in Appendix Table B-4.

[a] Ratio of total income to average consumer credit receivables.

[b] Ratio of consumer credit income to average consumer credit receivables.

cates the way in which charges are reduced as the size of the loan increases. The maximum charge on a $300 loan in Colorado is 3 per cent per month, while the maximum charge on a $700 loan is 3 per cent for the first $300, 1.5 per cent for the next $200, and 1 per cent for the remaining $200. Thus, the $700 loan costs $2.00 per $100 in the first month and the $300 loan costs $3.00 per $100.

The number of lending institutions offering services competing with those of consumer finance companies increased steadily as new credit unions were formed and as banks expanded into the personal loan field. The existence of strong competition in personal lending is widely recognized, but the impact of this competition on finance charges is not clear.

9

Individual companies may meet competition by rate adjustments, by changing the nature of the loans, or by improving services and customer relations.

Changes in the composition of the loans of consumer finance companies played only a minor role in the changes in average charges. Personal loans dominated the loans of these companies throughout the period studied so that changes in sales financing were not large enough to alter the over-all trend in average charges. Since the proportion of sales financing done by the nine sample companies from 1949 to 1959 declined fractionally, any effects from the shift in the type of business would be to raise average charges as sales finance contracts typically carry lower rates.

Components of Finance Charges

Gross finance charges cover the total expenses of the lender, including the cost of the owners' funds used in the business (lender's profit) and the share of the total charge paid to dealers. The distribution of these components for the nine sample companies in 1959 is shown on Table 2.

The principal expense items in consumer credit lending are investigating credit applications, maintaining records, seeking new business, and collecting loans. These operating costs differ widely from one company to another and depend upon the type of business conducted by the company, the type of service rendered, and the efficiency and skill of the management. The operating expenses of the sample companies amounted to three-fifths of the total finance charge and averaged $14.25 per $100 of outstanding credit. They ranged from a minimum of $11 per $100 to a maximum of $20 per $100 at individual companies.

The cost of the funds used in lending to consumers accounted for about 30 per cent of total finance charges. Funds were provided by the owners and obtained from the public or other financial institutions. The total cost of funds in 1959 averaged $6.89 per $100 of outstanding consumer credit. Of this amount, $2.92 was paid to stockholders or retained by the company for use as equity funds.

Operating Expenses

Salaries and the related expenses of personnel accounted for nearly half of all operating expenses of consumer finance companies in 1959 and amounted to $6.45 per $100 of outstanding credit. The importance of salary costs reflects the personalized service offered by the consumer finance industry with its multiple offices and direct lending operations.

10

TABLE 2

COMPONENTS OF GROSS FINANCE CHARGES ON CONSUMER CREDIT
AT CONSUMER FINANCE COMPANIES, 1959
(per $100 of average outstanding credit)

Item	Mean Distribution		Range of Ratios[a] (dollars)	
	Dollars	Per Cent	Maximum	Minimum
Gross finance charges[b]	24.04	100.0	--	--
Dealer's share of gross finance charges	.17	.6	--	--
Lender's gross revenue	23.87	99.4	31.58	20.02
Operating expenses	14.25	59.3	20.30	10.87
Salaries	6.45	26.9	7.90	4.95
Occupancy costs	1.09	4.5	1.57	.77
Advertising	.89	3.7	1.68	.27
Provision for losses	1.98	8.2	2.92	1.20
Other[c]	3.84	16.0	9.17	3.63
Nonoperating expenses	9.62	40.0	11.75	8.30
Cost of nonequity funds	3.97	16.5	5.49	2.94
Income taxes	2.73	11.4	4.46	2.06
Cost of equity funds (lender's profit)	2.92	12.1	4.35	1.55
Retained	.61	2.5	2.19	-.79
Dividends	2.31	9.6	3.79	1.22

Source: Nine-company sample.

a
    Components in columns for maximum and minimum ratios are not additive as ratios for individual items were taken from the statements of different companies.

b
    Includes all finance charges and fees collected on consumer credit activities. Charges for insurance are not included and the cost of free insurance provided to borrowers was deducted.

c
    Includes a wide variety of cost items, such as supplies, legal fees, insurance, etc., for which separate information could not be obtained from all companies.

Individual companies showed variations in salary costs from $5 to $8 per $100 of consumer loans.

Provision for losses was the next largest item of expense. Since these provisions represent the company's estimate of anticipated losses rather than actual losses, they are not an effective measure of costs in any particular year. During a period of expanding volume such as the 1950's, provisions for losses usually exceed actual losses because they represent

11

estimates based on expanding volume. In every year covered by the study, provisions for losses were larger than actual losses charged off (Table 3), but the relationship may be reversed in recession years or in years of large unanticipated losses. During the period covered by the study, provisions for losses averaged 13 per cent of total operating expenses, or nearly $2 per $100 of outstanding credit. Actual losses averaged only $1.45 per $100 during the same period.

Actual losses charged off (net of recoveries) varied widely from year to year with changes in economic conditions and the experience and policies of individual companies. The range of losses among different companies was large and apparently reflected differences in credit standards and collection policies. In 1959 actual losses among sample companies ranged from $.95 to $2.60 per $100 of outstanding consumer credit. In some years the highest loss rates were five to six times the lowest charge-off rate (Table 3).

TABLE 3

LOSSES AND PROVISION FOR LOSSES ON CONSUMER CREDIT
AT CONSUMER FINANCE COMPANIES, SELECTED YEARS
(dollars per $100 of average outstanding credit)

Year	Provision for Losses	Net Losses Charged Off	Range of Ratios in Net Losses Charged Off	
			Maximum	Minimum
1929	--	1.53	--	--
1933	--	3.61	--	--
1936	--	3.04	--	--
1949	2.03	1.47	2.73	.50
1950	2.13	1.42	2.71	.53
1951	1.88	1.51	3.01	.51
1952	1.86	1.38	2.07	.61
1953	1.81	1.43	2.16	.60
1954	1.79	1.50	2.17	.73
1955	1.84	1.39	1.86	.50
1956	1.70	1.15	1.62	.45
1957	1.72	1.39	2.20	.58
1958	2.02	1.71	2.78	.77
1959	1.98	1.70	2.60	.95

Source: Data for 1929–36 are based on tabulations of sample of 153 companies from Dauer's Comparative Operating Experience, Appendix B, p. 205. Data for 1949–59 are based on our nine-company sample.

12

Rent and maintenance of quarters for the multiple offices required by consumer finance company operations averaged $1 per $100 of outstanding consumer credit in 1959 and throughout the eleven years of the study. Individual companies reported variations between $.77 and $1.57 per $100 in 1959.

Advertising, an important element of cost in any business that must attract customers from the public, averaged 6 per cent of total operating costs, or 89 cents per $100 of outstanding loans in 1959. One company spent $1.68 per $100 of outstanding loans on advertising while another spent only 27 cents per $100.

The miscellaneous costs of lending operations were sizable and averaged $3.84, or 27 per cent of operating expenses. They included a wide range of items that had to be combined because comparable detail could not be obtained from all companies. The following detail from the accounting records of one company illustrates the nature of these costs: telephone and telegraph, postage and express, collection and appraisal, credit reports, printing and stationery, dues and subscriptions, legal and auditing, insurance, provision for depreciation, donations, taxes and license fees, and equipment and rental.

The operating expenses of consumer finance companies declined from 1949 to 1959 at about the same rate as the decline in gross finance charges, i.e., by about 10 per cent or $1.50 per $100 of outstanding credit, and continued to account for about 60 per cent of the gross finance charges. The downward trend in operating expenses during the 1950's was apparently a continuation of a longer-run trend. Data for 153 companies in a sample collected by the Russell Sage Foundation for the period 1929–39 showed a ratio of operating costs to outstanding consumer loans of 19 to 23 per cent, compared with ratios for the nine-company sample of between 14 and 16 per cent during the 1950's.[4] Separate information on the expenses of the two major companies lends supporting evidence of a decline in the per dollar costs of handling outstanding credit from the 1930's to the end of the 1950's.

The decline in total operating costs from 1949 to 1959 reflected decreases in all major expense items except provision for losses (Chart 2). The relative importance of various cost items to the nine consumer finance companies remained quite constant, except for expenditures on advertising, which dropped from 9 to 6 per cent of total expenses from 1949 to 1959.

[4] Dauer, *Comparative Operating Experience*, p. 201.

CHART 2
Operating Expenses on Consumer Credit at Consumer Finance Companies, 1949–59
(per $100 of average outstanding credit)

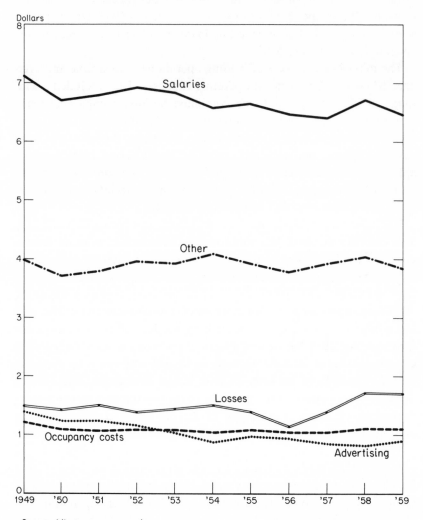

SOURCE: Nine-company sample.

Nonoperating Expenses

Nonoperating expenses, which include the cost of equity and nonequity funds and income taxes, made up 40 per cent of the gross finance charge at consumer finance companies in 1959. Although these expenses are part of the cost of providing credit to consumers, they are not exclusively related to consumer credit operations. They reflect the over-all organization and financial structure of the lending institution.

Nearly three-fourths of nonoperating expenses, or about $7 per $100 of outstanding credit, went into payments for the money used in the lending operations. About $4 of this total was paid to banks and other creditors and about $3 was paid out to stockholders or retained by the company.

Total nonoperating costs declined roughly in proportion to the decline in the gross finance charges and accordingly their share in the total remained relatively constant over the period under study. There were, however, some fundamental changes in the components of nonoperating expenses. The proportion paid for nonequity funds rose from 22 per cent in 1949 to 41 per cent in 1959 (see Chart 3). The share going to equity and to income taxes declined accordingly. This shift reflected in large part the increase in interest rates during this period and the greater dependence on nonequity financing.

SOURCES OF FUNDS

The total cost of funds as well as the distribution of payments between equity and nonequity sources depends in large part upon the financial structure of each company. The owners of the nine sample companies provided an average of 25 per cent of the funds used for their lending in 1959 and obtained the remaining 75 per cent from banks and the public (Table 4). The importance of equity funds, which had provided nearly a third of total resources in 1949, declined during the 1950's as the need for funds rose.

Banks were the principal source of short-term funds and provided 26 per cent of the total resources used by these companies. The proportion of bank borrowing varied widely, however, among individual institutions, ranging from a high of 42 per cent to a low of 7 per cent. Other short-term sources, principally commercial paper, accounted for about 7 per cent of the total resources. A few companies obtained small amounts from their employees in the form of thrift accounts or issued investment certificates.

CHART 3
Distribution of Nonoperating Expenses on Consumer Credit at Consumer Finance Companies, 1949–59

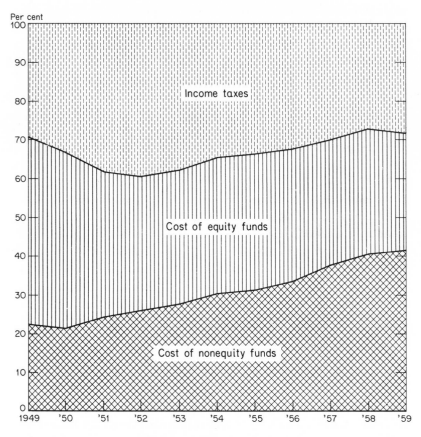

SOURCE: Nine-company sample. Based on data in Appendix Table B-4.

About 38 per cent of all funds was obtained from long-term sources—in the form of either senior or subordinated long-term obligations. The importance of long-term debt varied from 55 per cent at one company to 8 per cent at another. Subordinated debt was used by all but two of the companies and accounted for 15 per cent of the total resources of one company.

Senior long-term debt replaced bank loans as the principal source of nonequity funds during the 1950's. At the end of 1949 senior long-term obligations provided only 11 per cent of total resources and bank loans

16

TABLE 4

SOURCES OF FUNDS FOR CONSUMER FINANCE COMPANIES, END OF 1959
(per cent)

Item	Mean Distribution	Range of Ratios[a]	
		Maximum	Minimum
Debt, total	70.8	77.7	63.1
Short-term to banks	26.2	42.4	6.8
Other short-term[b]	7.1	20.4	0
Senior long-term	28.3	55.3	8.3
Subordinated	9.2	14.7	0
Dealer reserves	.3	1.3	0
Other liabilities	4.1	5.1	2.7
Total nonequity funds	75.2	82.8	70.1
Equity funds, total	24.8	32.3	17.2
Reserves	3.2	5.5	1.8
Preferred stock	3.7	5.2	0
Common stock and surplus	17.9	24.6	8.9
Total	100.0	--	--

Source: Nine-company sample.

a
    Components in columns for maximum and minimum ratios are not additive as ratios for individual items were taken from statements of different companies.

b
    Includes small amount of certificates of deposits and thrift accounts of employees.

provided 37 per cent. By the end of 1959, senior long-term debt provided 28 per cent of the total and bank loans 26 per cent.

A small proportion of the total funds available to consumer finance companies came from temporary sources such as dealer reserves or accounts payable. Although these funds are usually interest free, they add to the resources available to the company.

COST OF NONEQUITY FUNDS

The sample consumer finance companies paid an average of 5.0 per cent for interest-bearing debt outstanding in 1959. When accounts payable and other noninterest-bearing sources of funds are included, the average rate paid for nonequity funds was 4.6 per cent (Table 5). These rates understate the total cost of borrowing, however, when com-

17

TABLE 5

COST OF NONEQUITY FUNDS AT CONSUMER FINANCE COMPANIES, 1949–59
(per cent of average outstanding balances)

		Ratio of Dollar Cost of Nonequity Funds to		
Year	Debt	Total Nonequity Funds	Nonequity Funds Minus Nonearning Assets	Consumer Credit Receivables[a]
1949	3.0	2.8	3.7	2.3
1950	3.0	2.8	3.5	2.3
1951	3.2	3.0	3.7	2.5
1952	3.7	3.4	4.3	2.8
1953	3.8	3.5	4.4	2.9
1954	3.8	3.5	4.4	3.0
1955	3.7	3.4	4.3	3.0
1956	4.2	3.9	4.8	3.4
1957	4.6	4.3	5.2	3.8
1958	4.7	4.4	5.4	3.8
1959	5.0	4.6	5.6	4.0

Source: Nine-company sample.
[a] Based on the dollar share of total cost of nonequity funds allocated to consumer credit receivables by the ratio of consumer receivables to total earning assets.

pensating balances are required in connection with bank lines of credit. Banks customarily require finance companies to maintain a given percentage of their line on deposit with the bank. This requirement reduces the funds available to the finance company from the loan and increases the effective rate on the net amount obtained from the bank. The size of the required balance is set by individual agreement between the bank and finance company. Since the actual cost of compensating balance requirements cannot be calculated accurately because of the difficulty in estimating the change in working balances held, no attempt has been made to include these costs as part of the rate paid for funds. They are included here as part of the cost of nonearning assets.

The full cost of nonequity funds used in consumer lending includes part of the burden of providing funds used in nonearning forms, including compensating balances. This cost can be approximated by the ratio of interest paid for nonequity funds to total nonequity funds minus nonearning assets (Table 5, column 3). In 1959, nonearning assets added approximately 1 percentage point to the average cost of funds used in consumer lending.

Since equity sources provided part of the funds used for consumer lending, the cost of nonequity funds used in consumer lending expressed as a percentage of consumer credit receivables is less than the rate paid for funds. In 1959 about 25 per cent of funds were provided by equity sources so that the effective rate on the nonequity funds used for consumer lending was correspondingly reduced (Table 5, column 4).

The cost of nonequity funds used for consumer lending increased from 2.3 to 4 per cent of outstanding receivables between 1949 and 1959, reflecting higher rates on borrowed funds and decreased use of equity funds. The average rate paid on nonequity funds rose from 2.8 to 4.6 per cent and the proportion of equity funds used by consumer finance companies decreased from 32 per cent of total resources in 1949 to 25 per cent in 1959.

The cost of nonequity funds among the nine companies covered by the study showed a wide range both as a result of differences in rates paid on borrowed funds and differences in the proportion of nonequity funds used in their lending operations. The company with the lowest cost of funds paid an average 4.0 per cent for its nonequity funds in 1959 and obtained 70 per cent of its total funds from such sources. In contrast, the company with the highest cost of funds paid 6.2 per cent for its nonequity funds and obtained 74 per cent of its funds from such sources.

COST OF EQUITY FUNDS

The cost of equity funds used in consumer credit is a residual after other costs have been deducted from gross revenue. It represents that part of the lender's total return coming from consumer credit operations and is a real cost of credit in that it must be large enough to attract and hold risk capital in the industry. The lender's share in the total cost of consumer credit is an important element in his profit, but it is not the sole determinant. The profitability of a lending operation also depends upon the return from other earning assets, the cost of money, and the efficiency with which it is used. Consumer finance companies earned an average of $12.07 per $100 of net worth in 1959 while obtaining only $2.92 per $100 from the funds invested in consumer credit (Table 6, line 7, and Table 2, line 13).

The cost of equity funds to consumers declined from $4.97 per $100 of credit in 1949 to $2.92 per $100 in 1959. The decline was steady and

TABLE 6

FACTORS IN CONSUMER FINANCE COMPANY PROFITS, 1949-59

(per cent of average outstanding balances)

Ratio	1949	1950	1951	1952	1953	1954	1955	1956	1957	1958	1959
1. Net operating income from consumer credit to consumer receivables[a]	10.3	10.7	10.4	10.9	10.6	9.9	9.5	10.2	10.0	9.4	9.6
2. Net operating income to earning assets	10.8	11.2	10.9	11.5	11.2	10.5	10.4	11.0	10.9	10.2	10.4
3. Net operating income to total assets	9.1	9.5	9.3	9.8	9.6	8.9	8.9	9.5	9.3	8.9	9.1
4. Profits before taxes to equity funds	23.1	25.3	24.9	25.5	24.4	23.0	24.2	26.2	24.9	21.9	22.2
5. Net return from nonequity to equity funds (line 4 minus line 3)	14.0	15.8	15.6	15.7	14.8	14.1	15.3	16.7	15.6	13.0	13.1
6. Provision for income taxes to profit before taxes	36.8	41.6	48.9	52.3	51.1	48.5	46.9	47.0	45.7	43.4	45.8
7. Net profits to equity funds	14.5	14.8	12.7	12.2	12.0	11.9	12.8	13.9	13.5	12.4	12.1
8. Percentage of profit obtained from leverage on nonequity funds (line 5 ÷ line 4)	60.6	62.5	62.7	61.6	60.7	61.3	63.2	63.7	62.7	59.4	59.0
ALTERNATIVE DERIVATION OF LINE 5											
a. Net operating income to total assets (line 3) less	9.1	9.5	9.3	9.8	9.6	8.9	8.9	9.5	9.3	8.9	9.1
b. Cost of nonequity funds to nonequity funds equals	2.8	2.8	3.0	3.4	3.5	3.5	3.4	3.9	4.3	4.4	4.6
c. Net return from nonequity funds to nonequity funds times	6.3	6.7	6.3	6.4	6.1	5.4	5.5	5.6	5.0	4.5	4.5
d. Leverage coefficient (ratio of non-equity to equity funds) equals	2.2	2.4	2.5	2.5	2.5	2.6	2.8	3.0	3.1	3.0	3.0
e. Net return from nonequity to equity funds (line 5)[b]	13.9	16.1	15.8	16.0	15.3	14.0	15.4	16.8	15.5	13.5	13.5

[a] Equivalent to nonoperating expenses per $100 of average consumer credit receivables; see Table 2.

[b] Differences between lines 5 and e result from rounding errors introduced by alternative methods of calculation.

some decrease occurred in almost every year. The reasons for this decline can best be seen by examining the factors affecting the profits of the institution as a whole.

Lender's Rate of Profit

In addition to the return from consumer credit receivables, the lenders' profits also depend upon: the net return from other earning assets; the proportion of resources that are invested in earning assets; the financial advantage obtained from use of nonequity funds; and the applicable tax rates on net income.

RETURN ON OTHER EARNING ASSETS

All of the sample companies engaged in some activities other than lending to consumers such as providing insurance or lending to businesses. They earned 10.4 per cent on total receivables compared to an average of 9.6 per cent on consumer credit receivables in 1959 (Table 6). The higher rate of return on total receivables indicates that the average return on other assets was higher than on consumer credit receivables. Since other earning assets amounted to only 1.3 per cent of all earning assets, the average return per dollar of nonconsumer assets was obviously high. Not all of the companies in the sample showed this relationship, however. Five of the companies in the study in 1959 reported a higher return on total earning assets than on consumer credit; the other four showed fractionally higher returns on consumer credit.

Part of the high return on other earning assets may be explained by the difficulty of segregating the costs of handling insurance and other activities from the cost of consumer credit so that the quantitative results must be regarded with caution. The high indicated return on other activities, however, suggests the importance of these operations in the over-all profits of consumer finance companies.

COST OF NONEARNING ASSETS

The sample companies held 12.3 per cent of their assets in nonearning forms at the end of 1959. The amounts required for cash, bank balances, and other nonearning assets depend upon the number of offices, compensating balance requirements, and operating needs. The proportion of assets held in nonearning forms in 1959 ranged from 18 per cent at one company to 5.4 per cent at another.

These funds must be supplied either by borrowing or from equity sources and added to the over-all costs of the business. An indication of the costs involved can be obtained by comparing the net operating income on earning assets with the rate earned on total assets. The difference between these ratios is a measure of the loss of return that results from the incomplete employment of resources. In 1959, the sample companies showed a net operating income of 10.4 per cent on all earning assets and 9.1 per cent on total assets (Table 6).

The cost of nonearning assets varied widely from company to company reflecting differences in operating needs, in the efficiency of handling of cash balances, and in compensatory balance requirements. One company reported a spread of 2.4 per cent between the ratio of net operating income to earning assets and the rate on total assets, while the company with the smallest difference reported a spread of only 0.6 per cent.

FINANCIAL ADVANTAGE OF THE USE OF NONEQUITY FUNDS

If the lender can earn more on the funds that he invests than he pays for those he borrows, the difference increases the return on equity. This financial advantage or leverage from the use of nonequity funds is an essential part of the profits of most financing operations. The importance of income from this source to the return on equity depends upon the rate that can be earned on invested funds, the cost of nonequity funds, and the proportion of nonequity funds to equity funds.

Consumer finance companies were able to earn a net operating income of 9.1 per cent on the assets employed in the business before the cost of funds and taxes in 1959. If only equity funds were used in the business, this return would also be the return before taxes on equity funds. The net profits of these companies before taxes, however, amounted to 22.2 per cent of net worth. The difference in the return on equity and the return on total assets reflects the financial advantage of use of borrowed funds. About 60 per cent of returns before taxes could be traced to use of nonequity funds.

The part played by the cost of funds and ratio of nonequity to equity funds is shown in Table 6. Since the consumer finance companies were able to obtain nonequity funds at an average of 4.6 per cent and could clear 9.1 per cent on these funds, they were able to net 4.5 per cent on the nonequity funds used in the business. By using $3 of nonequity funds for every dollar of equity funds, they were able to earn three times 4.5 per cent, or 13.5 per cent, on equity funds by the use of borrowed funds. This return plus the normal return of 9.1 per cent on equity funds used in the business gave them a net profit before taxes of 22.6 per cent on equity funds.

INCOME TAXES

Consumer finance companies pay the regular federal income tax rates and state taxes. The information available in the financial statements of these companies indicates their provisions for taxes each year but does not show the cash payments. As a result, the data do not measure the actual payments in each year but show the impact of taxes over a period of time. Provision for taxes varied considerably from year to year and averaged 46 per cent of net operating income after interest during the eleven years 1949–59.

TREND IN LENDER'S PROFITS

The return on consumer credit receivables as measured by net operating income declined slightly from the early 1950's to 1959 (Table 6). The impact of this decline was largely offset, however, by a slight rise in return on other earning assets and by a reduction in nonearning assets. The sample companies were able to maintain a relatively stable return on total assets despite the slight decline in their principal source of income.

The major problem for consumer finance companies during this period was the maintenance of satisfactory profit levels in the face of increasing interest costs. The rate they paid for funds increased 65 per cent from 1949 to 1959. They tried to offset this additional cost by expanding their debt-equity ratios to maintain the financial advantages of the use of borrowed funds, but were only partly successful. In 1958 and 1959, the additions to profits from the use of nonequity funds fell substantially from earlier levels and profit rates declined accordingly.

Consumer finance companies typically pay a substantial part of their net profits to shareholders in the form of dividends. They paid out 60 per cent of net profits in 1959, which resulted in a return of 7.7 per cent to stockholders on the equity of the company. Since the market price of the stocks of most consumer finance companies was above the book value of the stocks in 1959, the return per share on the market value of the stock of these companies was below the return on the book value.

Comparison of Companies with Highest and Lowest Finance Charges

The number of companies that could be included in the sample was too small to permit the use of correlation analysis to examine the relationship between costs and individual factors determining these costs. A comparison of the experience of several companies showing consistently high average finance charges with those of companies showing low charges gives some indication of the reasons for the variations in charges.

23

To avoid the problem of unusual ratios that occur from year to year, averages of the data for eleven years were used in these comparisons. Although the two companies with the lowest charges were larger than the three companies with the highest charges, the sample was not large enough to establish a relationship between size and costs.

The finance charges on consumer credit in 1949-59 were consistently higher at three companies in the sample and consistently lower at two others. The difference between finance charges at the high- and low-charge companies averaged about 4.4 percentage points or about 25 per cent of the total finance charge (Table 7). Some of this difference probably reflected variations in the credit services to the consumer, although such differences are difficult to identify statistically.

The three companies with the highest charges apparently made more risky loans, as their actual loss ratios were 20 per cent higher than those of the companies with the lowest charges. The other costs associated with high-risk business, such as the additional attention required in screening loans and higher collection costs, add greatly to the operating expenses of companies handling high-risk loans. Every category of expense at the high-charge companies was higher except for nonoperating expenses. The principal differences occurred in salary and "other" expenses. One of the companies with low charges held a sizable amount of sales finance paper which typically carries lower rates and tends to lower many cost items. The other low-charge company, however, engaged almost entirely in personal lending, as did the three companies with highest charges.

The high-charge companies reported a lower net operating income on their consumer lending than the low-charge companies despite their higher charges. Their operating costs were 50 per cent higher than those of the companies with lowest charges although they averaged only 40 per cent more on their charges.

The high-charge companies were able to obtain more income from their insurance and other earning assets than the low-charge companies. The former earned 10.3 per cent on their total earning assets compared with 9 per cent on their consumer credit receivables. The low-charge companies, however, showed only a slightly higher return on total earning assets than on consumer credit receivables (Table 7).

Although consumers had to pay more for credit at the high-charge companies, the additional charges were absorbed by higher operating expenses incurred in providing credit to consumers. The profits of high-charge companies were smaller than those of the low-charge companies;

TABLE 7

COMPARISON OF CONSUMER FINANCE COMPANIES WITH HIGHEST
AND LOWEST AVERAGE FINANCE CHARGES, 1949-59[a]

Item	Three High-Charge Companies (1)	Two Low-Charge Companies (2)	Difference (col. 1 minus col. 2) (3)
DOLLARS PER $100 OF AVERAGE OUTSTANDING CONSUMER CREDIT			
Finance charges[b]	26.30	21.90	4.40
Operating expenses	17.30	11.40	5.90
Salaries	7.50	5.10	2.40
Occupancy costs	1.10	1.00	.10
Advertising	1.20	.90	.30
Provision for losses	2.30	1.60	.70
Actual losses	(1.60)	(1.30)	(.30)
Other	5.20	2.80	2.40
Nonoperating expenses (lender's net operating income from consumer credit receivables)	9.00	10.50	-1.50
SELECTED RATIOS (PER CENT)			
Total net operating income to all earning assets	10.3	10.8	-0.5
Cost of nonequity funds to total nonequity funds	3.7	3.4	.3
Nonequity to equity funds	2.6	2.7	-.1
Net profit to equity funds	12.4	12.8	-.4

[a]
All data are averages of annual individual company ratios for the eleven years 1949-59.
[b]
Excludes dealer share of gross finance charges.

the former averaged a return of 12.4 per cent on equity compared with an average of 12.8 per cent for the latter. The low-charge companies were able to show a higher profit largely because of the higher net operating income on their consumer credit business, and because of the greater financial advantage that resulted from a lower cost of nonequity funds and a slightly larger proportion of nonequity to equity funds.

25

TABLE 8

COMPARISON OF SELECTED HIGH- AND LOW-PROFIT CONSUMER
FINANCE COMPANIES, 1949-59[a]

Item	Two High-Profit Companies (1)	Three Low-Profit Companies (2)	Difference (col. 1 minus col. 2) (3)
SELECTED RATIOS (PER CENT)			
Net profit to equity funds	15.4	10.9	4.5
Net operating income on consumer credit receivables to consumer credit receivables	10.5	8.9	1.6
Total net operating income to all earning assets	12.1	9.7	2.4
Net operating income to total assets	10.1	8.0	2.1
Cost of nonequity funds to total nonequity funds	3.8	3.7	.1
Nonequity to equity funds	2.8	2.7	.1
DOLLARS PER $100 OF AVERAGE OUTSTANDING CONSUMER CREDIT			
Finance charges[b]	26.6	25.5	1.1
Operating expenses	16.1	16.6	-.5
Salaries	6.9	7.8	-.9
Occupancy costs	1.5	1.0	.5
Advertising	1.1	1.1	--
Provision for losses	2.0	2.2	-.2
Actual losses	(1.3)	(1.6)	(-.3)
Other	4.6	4.5	.1
Nonoperating expenses (lender's net operating income from consumer credit receivables)	10.5	8.9	1.6

a
All data are averages of annual individual company ratios for the eleven years 1949-59.
b
Excludes dealer share of the gross finance charges.

Comparison of High- and Low-Profit Companies

Two consumer finance companies in the sample consistently reported a higher return on net worth than the other companies and three companies were usually at the bottom of the profit scale.[5] The comparison of these two groups of companies suggests some of the differences in the nature of operations that contributed to the profit differential (Table 8). Both of the most profitable companies were larger than the three least profitable companies, but there were larger companies with lower profits and smaller companies with better profits at both extremes.

The most profitable companies averaged a return on equity of 15.4 per cent over the eleven years. This was 4.5 percentage points or 41 per cent better than the return of the low-profit companies. The profitable companies showed better experience in nearly all phases of their operations.

The profitable companies average 1.6 percentage points better than low-profit companies on their net operating income on consumer credit receivables. A comparison of earnings and operating expenses on consumer credit indicates that this advantage reflected both higher earnings and lower operating expenses. The profitable companies had salary expenses of almost 1 percentage point below those of the less profitable operations. Their occupancy costs, however, were higher, while their loss ratios were lower.

The profitable companies supplement their return on consumer credit with a higher return on their other earning assets. They reported a net operating income of 12.1 per cent on all earning assets, as opposed to the return for the less profitable companies of 9.7 per cent, thus increasing the earning spread from 1.6 to 2.4 percentage points.

The principal factor in the profits differential was the higher net operating income achieved by the profitable companies on their earning assets. Only minor differences appeared in the cost of funds and financial structure of the two groups.

---

[5] Two of the low-profit companies and one of the high-profit companies were also included in the preceding tabulation of companies with the highest and lowest finance charges.

CHAPTER 3
Sales Finance Companies

SALES finance companies engage primarily in buying instalment credit contracts secured by automobiles or other consumer goods from retailers. Since they deal initially with the merchants who sell the goods rather than with the consumers, they have been free from many of the legal limitations and restrictions that have been applied to direct lenders. Since 1935, however, a growing number of states have adopted laws that regulate various aspects of retail sales financing and place ceilings on finance charges. In general, sales finance companies are still subject to less detailed governmental supervision than other types of financial institutions extending credit to consumers.

Sales finance companies engage in a wide variety of activities other than purchasing consumer instalment credit contracts. All of the major companies finance inventories of the dealers who customarily sell them their consumer credit contracts. Some companies provide other types of financial aid to retailers; some engage in extensive insurance operations of nearly all types; some engage in a wide range of business financing; and a few have factoring or manufacturing subsidiaries. All of the companies covered by this study, however, obtained a large share of their income from automobile finance.

Sales finance companies held $10.1 billion in consumer credit at the end of 1959. They ranged in size from giant nationwide companies with assets of several billion dollars to companies owned by a single individual that held only a few thousand dollars in instalment paper. The study covers ten large companies that were willing and able to provide cost infomation. It does not necessarily present a complete picture of the cost of consumer credit in the sales finance industry as a whole. The companies in the sample account for a sizable segment of the industry, and at the end of 1959 held 83 per cent of the automobile paper of all sales finance companies. The sample is described in detail in Appendix A.

Diversification of Lending Activities

Consumer credit receivables accounted for 72 per cent of the total assets of the ten sample companies and 81 per cent of their earning assets (Table 9). Earning assets other than consumer credit receivables included instalment paper on industrial equipment, trucks, buses, and machinery; wholesale paper on automobiles, appliances, and industrial equipment; business loans; securities; and investments in many types of subsidiaries.

28

TABLE 9

USES OF FUNDS BY SALES FINANCE COMPANIES, END OF 1959
(per cent)

Item	Mean Distribution	Range of Ratios[a] Maximum	Minimum
Earning assets, net	88.6	95.4	83.5
Consumer credit	72.0	79.6	41.7
Automobile paper	52.9	77.3	28.3
Other goods paper	2.3	12.0	0
Personal loans	16.8	45.2	0
Other	16.6	50.9	6.6
Cash and bank balances	9.9	15.3	3.7
Other assets	1.5	2.9	.3
Total	100.0	--	--

Source: All data are averages of ratios for ten sample companies.

a
Components in columns for maximum and minimum ratios are not additive as ratios for individual items were taken from statements of different companies.

The companies covered by this study engaged primarily in automobile financing, which accounted for 53 per cent of their total assets. Other consumer goods paper on appliances, boats and mobile homes, etc., accounted for 2 per cent of their assets; and personal loans accounted for about 17 per cent.

Most of the personal loans made by these companies were made under state small-loan laws and were handled by consumer finance company subsidiaries. The distinction between a sales finance company and a consumer finance company is arbitrary in some cases because a company may engage in both types of business. A sales finance company has been defined for statistical purposes by the Federal Reserve System as any finance company that has more than half of its consumer receivables in sales finance paper. All but one of the sample companies made personal loans. One company reported 52 per cent of its consumer assets in personal loans at end of 1959 and would have been classified as a consumer finance company on that date. Its activities in earlier years justified its inclusion as a sales finance company.

Gross Finance Charges

Consumers paid approximately $15 per $100 for automobile loans at the ten sample sales finance companies in 1959.[1] Of this amount, one-fourth of the total was estimated to have been retained by dealers under participation agreements. The remaining three-fourths was retained by the finance companies.

The average charge at individual companies varied widely. The lowest average charge on automobile paper in 1959 was $11 per $100 of outstanding credit, while the highest was $20 per $100. Part of this difference reflected variations in the composition of their receivables rather than differences in rates on similar contracts. Since used-car paper and high-risk paper carry higher rates, companies that hold a relatively large portion of such contracts show a higher average rate of charge.

The average charge on new- and used-automobile credit (using the simple average for the ten companies) declined during the 1950's to a low in 1956, rising slightly during the next few years (Chart 4). The downward trend in average charges conceals divergent trends at individual companies within the sample. The companies with the lowest charges in 1949 showed a slight increase in average charges during the decade, while those with highest charges showed a sizable decline. Thus the decline in the over-all average reflects a reduction in the spread between companies with the highest and lowest charges rather than a general decline at all companies. Since the companies with the lowest charges also hold a large share of the automobile paper held by all sales finance companies, the over-all average weighted by the dollar size of each company shows a considerably smaller percentage decline than the simple average.

The changes in the average rates on all automobile paper as measured by the ratio of income to receivables do not correspond closely to the

[1] Charges quoted are approximations based on two methods of averaging the data from the ten sales finance companies. The simple average treats each company as a unit. The weighted average weights each company by its receivables. The relevant gross finance charges are:

	Simple Average			Weighted Average		
	1949	1959	Percentage Change	1949	1959	Percentage Change
Automobile paper	$20.40	$15.80	−23	$14.30	$13.70	−4
Personal loans	$25.00	$21.50	−14	$24.70	$22.40	−9

30

CHART 4
Gross Finance Charges on Consumer Credit at Sales Finance
Companies, by Type of Credit, 1949–59
(per $100 of average outstanding credit)

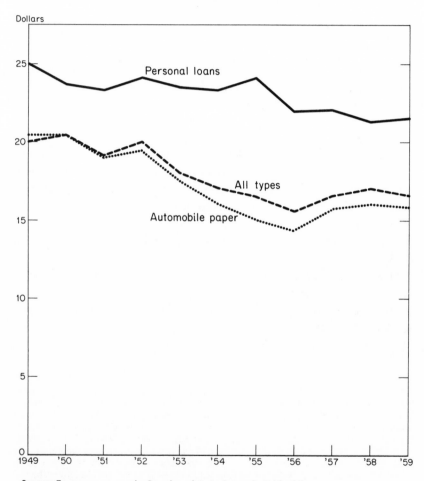

SOURCE: Ten-company sample. Based on data in Appendix Table C-5.

31

changes in rates indicated by a series of new-automobile rates developed from other sources as another part of the study.[2]

The rates paid for personal loans at sales finance companies were similar to those paid at consumer finance companies. Consumers paid about $22 per $100 for personal loans at sales finance companies in 1959, compared with an average of $24 per $100 at consumer finance companies in the same year. With one exception, the average rate paid at each individual sales finance company fell within the range of rates reported by the consumer finance companies. The trend in charges for personal loans at sales finance companies was also similar to that shown at consumer finance companies. The average charge on these loans at sales finance companies (using simple averages) declined by $3.50 per $100, or 14 per cent, from 1949 to 1959.

Components of Finance Charges

The gross finance charges at sales finance companies include the dealer's share of the charge, the lender's operating expenses, the cost of funds, including the owner's funds, and taxes (Table 10). The average finance charge on all types of consumer credit held in 1959 was $16.59 per $100 of outstanding credit. Of this total, an estimated $2.95 was retained by dealers,[3] leaving $13.64 per $100 as the lender's gross income from consumer credit.

Operating expenses of providing consumer credit accounted for the largest share of the total finance charge. They amounted to $7.74 or nearly one-half of the cost to the consumer in 1959. Since this figure includes the cost of handling sales finance paper, personal loans, and other goods paper, it understates the average cost of handling personal

---

[2] Robert P. Shay, *New Automobile Finance Rates, 1924–62*, NBER, OP 86, 1963. The two series are not directly comparable since they reflect differences in scope, coverage, and weighting procedures. The Shay new-auto finance rate series represents an average of rates paid by new-car purchasers at the time the credit contract is originated. Thus, its scope and coverage are narrower than the data presented here. Further, the Shay series represents average rates from four large companies *per credit contract* on *credit extended*. As noted in Chapter 1, data in this study are *simple company averages* of annual earnings per $100 of *average credit outstanding*. Thus, the series in this study is subject to the following influences that would not be reflected in the Shay series: (1) changes in the relative importance of new- and used-car contracts; (2) changes in rates on used-car contracts; (3) changes in the share of the finance charge retained by the dealer; (4) changes in rates charged by companies not included in Shay's sample; and (5) a time lag between changes in rates on contracts written and their effect upon the receipt of income relative to average credit outstanding.

[3] The gross finance charges and this estimate of the dealer's share of the gross charges are understated by the amount of any dealer's share on consumer goods other than automobiles, as no estimate was included for such amounts.

TABLE 10

COMPONENTS OF GROSS FINANCE CHARGES ON CONSUMER CREDIT
AT SALES FINANCE COMPANIES, 1959
(per $100 of average outstanding credit)

Item	Mean Distribution		Range of Ratios[a] (dollars)	
	Dollars	Per Cent	Maximum	Minimum
Gross finance charges[b]	16.59	100.0	--	--
Dealer's share of gross finance charges	2.95	17.8	--	--
Lender's gross revenue	13.64	82.2	17.69	9.55
Operating expenses	7.74	46.6	11.96	2.96
Salaries	3.47	20.9	5.13	1.59
Occupancy costs	.43	2.6	.82	.09
Advertising	.31	1.9	.81	.02
Provision for losses	1.46	8.8	2.35	.35
Other[c]	2.07	12.4	2.97	.88
Nonoperating expenses	5.90	35.6	7.16	2.99
Cost of nonequity funds	4.02	24.2	4.57	3.44
Income taxes	1.07	6.5	1.00	.47
Cost of equity funds (lender's profit)	.81	4.9	1.31	-1.11
Dividends	.48	2.9	.77	0
Retained	.33	2.0	.90	0

Source: Ten-company sample.

a
Components in columns for maximum and minimum ratios are not additive as ratios for individual items were taken from statements of different companies.

b
Includes all finance charges and fees collected on consumer credit
activities. Charges for insurance are not included and the cost of free
insurance provided to borrowers was deducted.

c
Includes a wide variety of cost items, such as supplies, legal fees,
insurance, etc., for which separate information could not be obtained from
all companies.

loans and overstates the average cost of handling automobile paper.
The average cost of handling personal loans at consumer finance companies was $14.42 or nearly twice the average operating costs at sales
finance companies. If the consumer finance cost figure is used to estimate the cost of handling personal loans at sales finance companies, the
derived cost of handling sales finance paper was only $5.26 per $100 of
outstanding credit.[4]

[4] See Table 30.

The average operating costs of consumer credit at individual sales finance companies ranged from $2.96 to $11.96 per $100 of outstandings. Part of this differential reflects differences in importance of personal loan activities. When the extreme ratios are adjusted by an estimate of the cost of handling personal loans, the gap narrows slightly, but the range is still sizable. This difference indicates wide variations in the type of receivables held and efficiency of the sales finance company operations.

The cost of funds, both equity and nonequity, accounted for 29 per cent of total consumer credit costs and amounted to $4.83 per $100 outstanding in 1959. These costs include interest payments on borrowed funds, dividend payments to the owners, and the share of net profits retained in the business. Payments for nonequity funds accounted for four-fifths of the total cost of funds in 1959. The spread in costs of funds among individual companies was small relative to the spread in operating expenses. The cost of nonequity funds at individual companies ranged from $4.57 to $3.44 per $100 of outstanding credit.

Operating Expenses

Salaries and wages account for nearly half of the total operating expenses of handling consumer credit receivables at sales finance companies. They averaged $3.47 per $100 of credit outstanding in 1959. Individual company variations were sizable, ranging from $1.59 to $5.13. Part of this range reflects variations in the type of credit handled and, in particular, the extent of their personal loan operations. When the salary costs of the highest- and lowest-cost companies were adjusted for an estimate of expenses of personal loan operations, the variations in salary expense were reduced but were still sizable. The wide spread in salary cost suggests major differences in the nature of sales financing operations among individual companies.

Salary expenses declined during the period studied despite the rise in wage rates and employee benefits that characterized this period. A low was reached in 1956 when salary costs were $3.12 per $100 of credit, compared with an average of $4.16 in 1949 and $3.47 in 1959 (Chart 5). Despite this decline, salary expenses accounted for about the same percentage of total operating expenses throughout the period. A number of influences may have contributed to the reduction of salary expenses. The average contract size more than doubled from 1949 to 1959, thus reducing the handling costs in relation to the dollar volume. Improved operating procedures and the increased use of electronic tabulating and bookkeeping equipment probably also helped to reduce personnel costs.

CHART 5
Operating Expenses on Consumer Credit at Sales Finance
Companies, 1949–59
(per $100 of average outstanding credit)

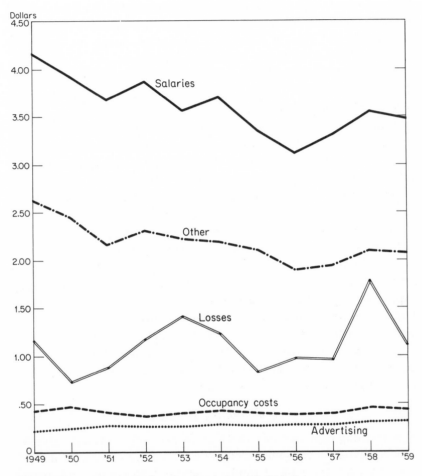

SOURCE: Ten-company sample. Based on data in Appendix Table C-4.

Losses are an unavoidable expense of sales finance operations and
provisions for losses represented a sizable item of expense. In 1959,
sales finance companies set aside about 19 per cent of total operating
expenses for potential losses. Since these provisions represent the companies' judgment of the range of possible losses, they do not reflect the
actual loss experience from year to year. Provisions for losses exceeded

35

actual losses (net of recoveries) during every year of the study except 1958. In 1959 actual losses amounted to $1.11 per $100 of receivables or about three-fourths of the total provisions for losses. Individual company differences in losses and in provision for losses were sizable. Actual losses ranged from $.21 to $1.66 in 1959 and provisions for losses ranged from $.35 to $2.35. These differences suggest considerable variation in the quality and type of paper that is handled among the individual companies and in the nature of recourse agreement.

Advertising and occupancy costs are a comparatively small part of the total operating expense for sales finance companies as they deal primarily with auto dealers or other retailers rather than directly with the public. They do not need numerous or expensive locations for the success of their operations. Many promotional costs are incurred as part of their regular operations and show up as personnel costs and other expenses, rather than as separate advertising or promotional expenses. Their advertising costs amounted to only 31 cents per $100 of credit in 1959 and costs of quarters amounted to only 43 cents per $100. These costs remained relatively stable throughout the period.

Many of the expenses of the sales finance companies could not be tabulated separately because of the lack of uniform accounting. These unclassified items, which accounted for 27 per cent of total operating expenses in 1959, included such items as auditing, credit reports, donations, taxes (other than income), fidelity bonds, insurance, legal bills, postage, telephone, telegraph, travel, depreciation, recording fees, and others. The total of these miscellaneous expenses declined from $2.63 per $100 of receivables in 1949 to $2.07 per $100 in 1959 (Table 10) but the changes in composition could not be traced.

Nonoperating Expenses

Nonoperating expenses accounted for 36 per cent of the average gross finance charge on consumer credit at sales finance companies in 1959. They included the cost of funds, equity and nonequity, and income taxes. The cost of nonequity funds made up more than two-thirds of these costs with the remainder split almost evenly between the cost of equity funds (lender's profit) and provisions for income taxes.

The amount of nonoperating expenses as well as the relative importance of these expenses in the total cost of credit varied considerably from year to year without any clear-cut trend. Among components of nonoperating expenses, the cost of nonequity funds increased in importance from 40 per cent in 1949 to 68 per cent in 1959. The share going to equity funds and for income taxes dropped accordingly (Chart 6).

CHART 6
Distribution of Nonoperating Expenses on Consumer Credit at Sales Finance Companies, 1949–59

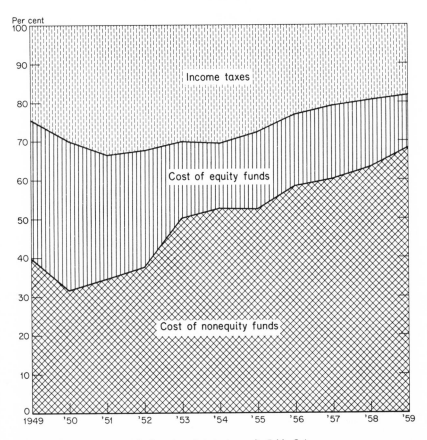

SOURCE: Ten-company sample. Based on data in Appendix Table C-4.

SOURCES OF FUNDS

The cost of funds, as well as the distribution of payments between equity and nonequity sources, depends in large part upon the financial structure of the company. During 1949, equity funds provided an average of 19 per cent of the total resources of the sample sales finance companies. They declined in importance, however, as a source of funds during the period and by the end of 1959 accounted for only 15 per cent of the total (Table 11).

All of the major credit markets were tapped by sales finance companies to obtain funds for their rapid growth during the 1950's. Banks

TABLE 11

SOURCES OF FUNDS FOR SALES FINANCE COMPANIES, END OF 1959
(per cent)

Item	Mean Distribution	Range of Ratios[a]	
		Maximum	Minimum
Debt, total	78.5	82.7	73.2
Short-term to banks	29.8	46.9	2.9
Other short-term	16.6	33.9	9.7
Senior long-term	21.0	49.5	8.9
Subordinated	11.1	16.6	8.8
Dealer reserves	1.8	3.2	.7
Other liabilities	4.6	9.3	1.3
Total nonequity funds	84.9	91.5	82.4
Equity funds, total	15.1	17.6	8.5
Reserves	2.0	4.3	1.1
Preferred stock	2.7	4.6	0
Common stock and surplus	10.4	13.9	6.2
Total	100.0	--	--

Source: Ten-company sample.
a
   Components in columns for maximum and minimum ratios are not
additive as ratios for individual items were taken from statements
of different companies.

provided the largest share, although the importance of bank borrowing declined during the period. At the end of 1959 bank loans accounted for 30 per cent of the total resources of the sample companies compared to 50 per cent at the end of 1948.

The importance of bank borrowing among individual companies ranged from 3 to 47 per cent of total resources at the end of 1959. Commercial paper markets provided funds to supplement bank credit. Although separate figures were not collected on commercial paper, it accounted for most of the nonbank short-term debt, which amounted to 17 per cent of total resources at the end of 1959.

The anticipated growth of financing needs and changing money market conditions brought about a wider use of long-term debt during the 1950's. Senior long-term debt increased as an average source of funds from 7 to 22 per cent of total resources from 1949 to 1959. One company reported that nearly half of its total funds were obtained from senior long-term sources. At the other extreme, another company reported only 9 per cent from these sources.

Subordinated debt plays a dual role in the financing of consumer lending. It provides nonequity funds and serves as a base for the expansion of other borrowing. The expanding needs of sales finance companies for nonequity funds combined with institutional interest in high-yield securities led to the increased use of subordinated debt. This type of debt supplied 11 per cent of total resources in 1959 compared with only 7 to 8 per cent in the early 1950's. Subordinated debt was used by all of the companies covered by the study and ranged in importance from 9 to 17 per cent of their total resources in 1959.

Miscellaneous liabilities and dealer reserves provide a steady source of noninterest-bearing funds for finance companies. Dealer reserves, or the amounts retained by the finance company as protection against possible losses, averaged 1.8 per cent of total resources of the sample companies at the end of 1959. Other liabilities accounted for another 4.6 per cent, bringing the total of noninterest-bearing sources of funds to 6.4 per cent of total resources.

COST OF NONEQUITY FUNDS

The cost of nonequity funds averaged $4.02 per $100 of outstanding consumer credit in 1959, or 24 per cent of the gross finance charge at sales finance companies. These costs depend upon the rate paid for these funds and the proportion of nonequity funds used in financing consumer receivables. In 1959 sales finance companies paid an average rate of 4.5 per cent for borrowed funds. The effective rate on all nonequity funds including noninterest-bearing liabilities was 4.2 per cent. This rate understates the total cost of borrowing, however, because it does not allow for the reduction in usable funds that results from compensating balance requirements. Bank requirements for sales finance companies are similar to those discussed for consumer finance companies in the previous chapter. The costs of compensating balances and other non-earning assets added about .5 of a percentage point to the cost of funds used in lending to consumers in 1959 (Table 12).

The amounts of nonequity funds required for consumer lending are reduced by the use of equity funds, however, which reduces the effective cost of these funds per $100 of consumer credit. The sample sales finance companies obtained about 16 per cent of their resources from equity sources and the effective cost of nonequity funds was reduced accordingly, as indicated by the difference between columns 3 and 4 of Table 12.

The cost of nonequity funds as a percentage of consumer credit receivables rose from 2.6 to 4.0 per cent from 1949 to 1959, primarily as

39

TABLE 12

COST OF NONEQUITY FUNDS AT SALES FINANCE COMPANIES, 1949-59
(per cent of average outstanding balances)

		Ratio of Dollar Cost of Nonequity Funds to		
Year	Debt	Total Nonequity Funds	Nonequity Funds Minus Nonearning Assets	Consumer Credit Receivables[a]
1949	3.0	2.6	3.2	2.6
1950	3.0	2.6	3.2	2.5
1951	3.3	2.9	3.4	2.7
1952	3.5	3.1	3.6	2.9
1953	3.9	3.4	4.1	3.3
1954	3.7	3.3	3.9	3.2
1955	3.6	3.3	3.9	3.1
1956	4.1	3.7	4.4	3.5
1957	4.5	4.1	4.7	4.0
1958	4.3	3.9	4.6	3.7
1959	4.5	4.2	4.8	4.0

Source: Ten-company sample.
a
Based on the dollar share of the total cost of nonequity funds allocated to consumer credit receivables by the ratio of consumer receivables to total earning assets.

a result of an increase in rates paid for funds. Sales finance companies paid an average of 4.5 per cent for money in 1959 compared with 3.0 per cent in 1949. At the same time the proportion of equity funds dropped from 18.6 to 15.8 per cent of total resources.

COST OF EQUITY FUNDS

The cost of equity funds (lender's profit) averaged only 5 per cent of the gross finance charge on consumer credit in 1959. This element of cost declined sharply as a proportion of both the finance charge and non-operating expenses during the period covered by the study (Chart 6). The cost of equity funds used in consumer lending fell from a high of $2.97 per $100 of credit in 1950 to the low of 81 cents per $100 in 1959. The decline was fairly steady and resulted from a decline in the proportion of equity capital used and from an increase in interest rates. The nature of this decline can best be seen in the perspective of the factors affecting the over-all profits of sales finance companies.

Lender's Rate of Profit

As noted in Chapter 2, the return that a lender obtains on net worth or equity funds depends upon all phases of the companies' operations: the net return on consumer credit; the net return from other activities (which may be related or unrelated to consumer credit activities); the proportion of resources that is invested; the financial advantage that can be achieved through the use of borrowed funds; and the income tax rates.

RETURN FROM OTHER EARNING ASSETS

In addition to their consumer credit operations, all of the sales finance companies in the sample engaged in some other activities. They all provided wholesale financing for retailers and wrote some types of insurance. In addition, some of them engaged in a variety of other financial and industrial activities. The sample companies showed a larger average net operating return on their total earning assets than they did on their consumer credit receivables in every year covered. In 1959, all but one of the sample companies showed a larger return on all earning assets than on their consumer credit receivables.[5]

Other activities may be tied in with their consumer credit business or may be completely unrelated. A company that sells the accident insurance on automobiles and lends the money on the same cars can consider the combined return from both activities in establishing its policies. Such a company may reduce its rates on its consumer credit without sacrificing profits if it can gain on its insurance.

COST OF NONEARNING ASSETS

The ten sample companies held 11.4 per cent of their total assets in nonearning forms at the end of 1959; 10 per cent was in cash and bank balances and the remainder in other forms.

The cash requirements of sales finance companies are determined by their operating needs, the number of offices and compensating balances required by their creditors. These funds must be supplied either by borrowing or from equity funds and are a cost of doing business. The imputed costs of nonearning assets can be approximated by the difference between the return on total assets and the return on earning assets. In recent years this spread has averaged slightly less than 1 percentage

---

[5] See the corresponding section in Chapter 2 for a discussion of the problems involved in estimating the return on assets other than consumer receivables.

point on total assets for the sample companies. The most efficient company in this respect managed to hold the costs of nonearning assets to about .3 of a percentage point. At the other extreme, nonearning assets cost one company 1.3 percentage points.

FINANCIAL ADVANTAGE OF THE USE OF NONEQUITY FUNDS

When the lender can earn a higher rate of return on the funds he invests than he pays for the funds he borrows, the differential accrues to the owners. This financial advantage from the use of nonequity funds is an important element in the profitability of sales financing operations. The sample sales finance companies earned an average of 6.3 per cent on total assets in 1959 before the cost of funds and income taxes (Table 13). The net profits before taxes of these companies, however, amounted to 18 per cent of equity funds, nearly three times the rate earned on total resources. Thus, nearly 65 per cent of their profits could be traced to the financial advantage of using nonequity funds. The sample sales finance companies were able to obtain nonequity funds at an average rate of 4.2 per cent and were able to earn 6.3 per cent on these funds, or a net of 2.1 per cent. They employed $5.6 of nonequity funds for every dollar of equity funds so that they were able to earn 2.1 per cent times 5.6, or 11.8 per cent, on their equity funds from the use of nonequity. This return, plus the average return on total resources of 6.3 per cent, equals the return on equity of 18 per cent (see the lower panel of Table 13).

The sample companies set aside an average of 45.5 per cent of the net profits before taxes as provision for tax payments during the eleven years covered by the study. The reported amount varied considerably from year to year as the allowance reflected adjustment for under- or overestimates and for special tax situations. After taxes, the sample companies earned an average of 10.3 per cent on their equity funds with individual companies showing variations between 7 and 14 per cent.

TREND IN LENDER'S PROFITS

The rate of profit on equity funds declined in the late 1950's and averaged less than 11 per cent in the last three years of the study, compared with an average of over 15 per cent in the first three years. The decline reflects the increase in the cost of nonequity funds and a decline in net operating income from consumer credit, which resulted in a slight decline in net operating income from total assets. Although the return on total assets varied from year to year, the average in the late 1950's was below that in the earlier years. The effects of this decline in return

42

TABLE 13

FACTORS IN SALES FINANCE COMPANY PROFITS, 1949–59

(per cent of average outstanding balances)

Ratio	1949	1950	1951	1952	1953	1954	1955	1956	1957	1958	1959
1. Net operating income from consumer credit to consumer receivables[a]	6.5	7.8	7.8	7.8	6.6	6.0	5.9	6.1	6.6	5.9	5.9
2. Net operating income to earning assets	7.8	9.0	8.5	8.5	8.2	8.1	7.5	7.3	7.6	7.0	7.2
3. Net operating income to total assets	6.4	7.6	7.3	7.3	7.1	7.1	6.6	6.4	6.6	6.1	6.3
4. Profits before taxes to equity funds	23.6	30.6	27.9	28.1	26.9	27.3	25.7	22.7	21.7	18.7	17.9
5. Net return from nonequity to equity funds (line 4 minus line 3)	17.2	23.0	20.6	20.8	19.8	20.2	19.1	16.3	15.1	12.6	11.6
6. Provision for income taxes to profit before taxes	37.6	41.9	47.3	48.7	50.0	50.3	48.4	46.6	45.0	43.1	42.5
7. Net profits to equity funds	14.7	17.6	14.4	14.1	13.4	13.5	13.2	12.1	11.9	10.5	10.3
8. Percentage of profit obtained from leverage on nonequity funds (line 5 ÷ line 4)	72.9	75.2	73.8	74.0	73.6	74.0	74.3	71.8	69.1	67.4	64.8
ALTERNATIVE DERIVATION OF LINE 5											
a. Net operating income to total assets (line 3)	6.4	7.6	7.3	7.3	7.1	7.1	6.6	6.4	6.6	6.1	6.3
less											
b. Cost of nonequity funds to nonequity funds	2.6	2.6	2.9	3.1	3.4	3.3	3.3	3.7	4.1	3.9	4.2
equals											
c. Net return from nonequity funds to nonequity funds	3.8	5.0	4.4	4.2	3.7	3.8	3.3	2.7	2.5	2.2	2.1
times											
d. Leverage coefficient (ratio of nonequity to equity funds)	4.6	4.8	4.9	5.1	5.6	5.7	6.0	6.2	6.1	5.7	5.6
equals											
e. Net return from nonequity to equity funds (line 5)[b]	17.5	24.0	21.6	21.4	20.7	21.7	19.8	16.7	15.3	12.5	11.8

[a] Equivalent to nonoperating expenses per $100 of average consumer credit receivables, see Table 10.

[b] Differences between lines 5 and e result from rounding errors introduced by alternative methods of calculation.

on profits was accentuated by the sharp rise in interest rates paid for nonequity funds. The average rate paid for nonequity funds increased by 62 per cent during the eleven years of the study. An increase in the ratio of nonequity to equity funds increased the leverage from the use of nonequity funds, but the high cost and lower return more than offset the gain obtained through the higher leverage, and the profit rate fell accordingly (Table 13).

The success of individual companies in maintaining their profit margins differed. All of the sample companies showed a lower return on equity toward the end than at the beginning of the decade. In 1959 net profits varied from a maximum of nearly 14 per cent of equity to a low of 7.8 per cent, while in 1950, the year of peak profits, the range was from a high of 26 to a low of 11 per cent.

Sales finance companies typically pay a substantial part of their net profits to shareholders in the form of dividends. In 1959 they paid out 57 per cent of their profits in dividends on preferred and common stock. The return to the common stockholders amounted to 5.9 per cent on the book value of the stock. Since the market price of stocks of most sales finance companies was above the book value of the stock in 1959, the return per share on market value of the stock was below that indicated for book value.

Comparison of High- and Low-Profit Companies[6]

None of the sales finance companies in the sample showed a consistently high ratio of net profit to equity throughout the entire period of the study. Similarly, no company showed a consistently low profit during the entire period. During the four years 1956–59, however, two companies were consistently in the highest position and two other companies were consistently among the three lowest companies in terms of profits. The two most profitable companies were among the largest companies, while the two least profitable were among the smallest companies in the sample.

The high-profit companies averaged a return of 14.7 per cent on their equity funds during the four years 1956–59. This was 5.5 percentage points above the profit rate for the low-profit companies (Table 14). The difference in profits arose almost entirely from the financial structure of

---

[6] The diversification of consumer credit activities among the sample sales companies made it impossible to make a meaningful comparison of companies showing the highest and lowest average finance charges similar to that shown in Chapter 2 for consumer finance companies.

TABLE 14

SELECTED RATIOS OF HIGH- AND LOW-PROFIT SALES FINANCE COMPANIES, 1956-59[a]
(per cent)

Ratio	Two High-Profit Companies (1)	Two Low-Profit Companies (2)	Difference (col. 1 minus col. 2) (3)
1. Net operating income from consumer credit to consumer receivables	6.1	6.1	--
2. Net operating income to earning assets	6.5	7.5	-1.1
3. Net operating income to total assets	6.2	6.3	-.1
4. Cost of nonequity funds to nonequity funds	3.6	4.1	-.5
5. Net return on nonequity funds to nonequity funds (line 3 minus line 4)	2.6	2.2	.4
6. Leverage coefficient (ratio of nonequity to equity funds)	9.3	5.1	4.2
7. Return from nonequity funds to equity funds (line 5 times line 6)	24.2	11.2	13.0
8. Net profit before taxes to equity funds[b]	29.0	18.0	11.0
9. Income taxes to equity funds	14.3	8.8	5.5
10. Net profit to equity funds	14.7	9.2	5.5

a
All data are averages for the four years 1956-59.
b
The ratio of net profits before taxes to equity funds in line 8 differs from the ratio derived by adding lines 7 and 3 because of rounding differences involved in the two methods of calculation.

the two groups rather than from their lending operations. Both groups of companies showed the same net operating income on consumer assets. The less profitable companies reported somewhat higher earnings on total earning assets but only a slightly larger return on total assets than the high-profit companies.

The high-profit companies were able to earn more than twice as much on their nonequity funds as the less profitable companies (Table 14, line 7). This rate of return was achieved by the more extensive use of debt financing and the less expensive funds. The high-profit companies paid .5 of a percentage point less for their nonequity funds than the less profitable companies and they used nearly twice as much debt relative to equity. The high-profit companies reported an average ratio of nonequity to equity funds of 9.3 compared with 5.1 for the other group. The financial advantage of using a high ratio of debt and low-cost funds permitted the high-profit companies to show an average profit before taxes of 29 per cent on equity for the four years 1955–59, 11 percentage points higher than the return reported by the two low-profit companies.

CHAPTER 4

Commercial Banks

COMMERCIAL banks are distinguished from other financial institutions primarily by their acceptance of demand deposits. Deposits provide them with funds but their responsibility for the liquidity and safety of the deposits limits the use of these funds. The privilege of receiving deposits is accompanied by an elaborate framework of legal and supervisory controls designed to protect depositors and govern the monetary effects of demand deposits. In addition, most states have adopted laws that set ceiling rates on various types of consumer credit extended by commercial banks.

Consumer credit is a relatively new and, in most cases, still a minor outlet for the funds of banks. Commercial banks held $18.8 billion of consumer credit at the end of 1959, but this amounted to only 10 per cent of their total loans and investments. The importance of consumer credit at individual banks varies widely. Some smaller banks specialize in consumer lending and place a large part of their loan portfolios in consumer credit. Many larger banks view consumer credit as a promising new outlet for funds, but in most cases it represents only a small part of their over-all lending.

The study was necessarily limited to data obtained from a small number of banks. Although information was obtained from fourteen banks, only nine of these could provide enough detailed cost information to be included in the major tabulations. The banks covered by the study were all relatively large. Several of them were among the largest hundred banks and all of them had total deposits of over $100 million. Although they had large consumer credit operations, the outstanding amount of consumer credit at the sample banks accounted for only 7 per cent of the total at all commercial banks. The sample is described in greater detail in Appendix A.

Diversification of Lending Activities

Consumer credit accounted for only 6 per cent of the total assets of the sample of commercial banks at the end of 1959 (Table 15). Commercial and industrial loans dominated their loan portfolios, but they held other loans of many types, U. S. government securities, and municipal and state obligations.

Some of the banks tended to specialize in one or two types of consumer lending, but most of them engaged in nearly all of the major types of consumer credit. They purchased indirect automobile paper and

TABLE 15

USES OF FUNDS BY COMMERCIAL BANK SAMPLE, END OF 1959
(per cent)

Item	Mean Distribution	Range of Ratios[a] Maximum	Minimum
Earning assets, net	74.0	81.8	66.2
Consumer credit	5.7	12.2	1.3
Automobile paper, direct	1.4	7.8	0
Automobile paper, indirect	1.4	6.9	0
Other goods paper	.4	1.2	0
Modernization loans	.9	2.2	0
Personal loans	1.6	2.7	.6
Other	68.3	75.4	60.3
Cash and bank balances	24.5	31.9	16.8
Other assets	1.5	2.0	.8
Total	100.0	--	--

Source: Nine-bank sample.
a
    Components in columns for maximum and minimum ratios are not additive as ratios for individual items were taken from statements of different companies.

other contracts from dealers, made direct loans on automobiles and appliances, made repair and modernization loans, and extended direct personal loans of all types. In addition, their retail departments usually extended instalment credit to businesses to finance machinery, equipment, and other facilities.

Nearly half of their consumer credit was extended for the purchase of automobiles. Their lending on automobiles was split almost evenly between direct and indirect financing. About half of the sample banks held both direct and indirect automobile paper. The others concentrated either in direct or indirect automobile financing.

All of the banks in the sample reported some personal loans. The importance of these loans in their portfolio ranged from 51 per cent of total consumer credit outstanding at one bank to 11 per cent at another. All but one of the banks reported some repair and modernization loans and some indirect lending on appliances and other consumer goods.

Gross Finance Charges

Gross finance charges averaged $10 per $100 on the consumer credit outstanding at commercial banks in 1959. This average covers a wide variety of rates on many different types of loans. The average finance charge by type of loan ranged from about $11.15 per $100 on appliance and other consumer goods paper to $8.79 per $100 on direct automobile loans (Chart 7).[1] Individual banks showed variations in charges from $5.60 to $15.00 per $100 of outstanding credit, with both the lowest and highest rate being reported on modernization loans.

Since the average finance charge includes an estimate of the amount retained by automobile dealers, these rates overstate the banks' gross income. The dealers' share of the charge amounted to an estimated 62 cents per $100 on the average charge for all types of credit and to $2.70 per $100 on indirect automobile financing.

The average finance charge at commercial banks increased 16 per cent over the five-year period 1955–59 (Chart 7), reflecting an increase both in the average rate on all types of credit, except direct automobile loans, and in the importance of personal loans in the loan mix. The average rate on personal loans increased about 15 per cent from 1955 to 1959, and these loans expanded from 17 to 28 per cent of the total consumer credit held by the sample banks. The rates on both other goods paper and modernization loans also rose sharply during this five-year period, the latter from $6.59 to $9.02 per $100 of outstanding loans.

Components of Finance Charges

The gross finance charge includes the amount retained by dealers, the lenders' operating expenses, the cost of funds, and income taxes (Table 16). The determination of these components at banks is complicated by the wide scope of their operations and by the difficulties of separating the costs of any particular type of credit. Much of the information from the sample banks was based on cost accounting systems that imply judgments about the allocation of costs among various functions. Averages based on these records indicated that 42 per cent of the total finance charge at banks went into operating expenses, 6 per cent into payments to dealers, and 52 per cent into the cost of the money and taxes. Operating expenses included the salaries of people handling consumer loans, charges for space used for consumer credit activities, advertising costs, provision for losses, and the many other day-to-day expenses associated with consumer credit operations.

The cost of money included the cost of handling deposits, as well as interest payments and the cost of equity, or the bank's profit. In 1959

---

[1] Weighted averages based on the dollar size of outstanding credit of each type at each bank show somewhat different levels and trends in charges (see Table 35).

CHART 7

Gross Finance Charges on Consumer Credit at Commercial Banks,
by Type of Credit, 1955–59
(per $100 of average outstanding credit)

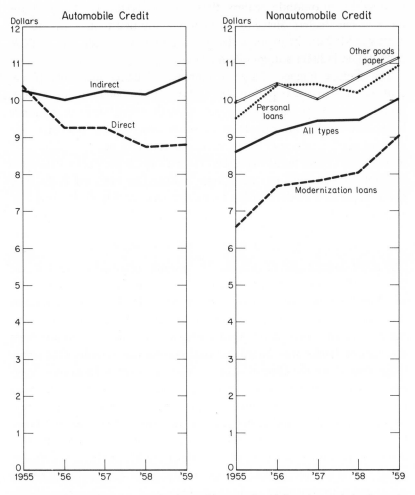

SOURCE: All types based on nine-bank sample; types of credit based on eight-bank sample.
Based on data in Table 35.

TABLE 16

COMPONENTS OF GROSS FINANCE CHARGES ON CONSUMER CREDIT
AT COMMERCIAL BANKS, 1959
(per $100 of average outstanding credit)

	Mean Distribution		Range of Ratios[a] (dollars)	
Item	Dollars	Per Cent	Maximum	Minimum
Gross finance charges[b]	10.04	100.0	--	--
Dealer's share of gross finance charges	.62	6.0		
Lender's gross revenue	9.42	94.0	12.30	6.78
Operating expenses	4.17	41.6	5.84	2.08
Salaries	2.33	23.2	3.25	1.28
Occupancy costs	.23	2.3	.36	.12
Advertising	.34	3.4	.79	.11
Provision for losses	.28	2.8	.42	.08
Actual losses	(.15)	(1.5)	(.28)	(.08)
Other	.99	9.9	1.69	.16
Nonoperating expenses	5.25	52.4	8.49	2.81
Cost of nonequity funds	1.50	15.0	2.35	.71
Income taxes	1.33	13.3	2.07	.70
Cost of equity funds (lender's profit)	2.42	24.1	4.40	.57
Dividends	1.49	14.8	3.19	.34
Retained	.93	9.3	2.14	0

Source: Nine-bank sample.

a
Components in columns for maximum and minimum ratios are not additive as ratios for individual items were taken from statement of different companies.

b
Includes all finance charges and fees collected on consumer credit activities. Charges for insurance are not included and the cost of free insurance provided to borrowers was deducted.

the average cost of nonequity funds amounted to $1.50 per $100 of outstanding credit, about 15 per cent of the average finance charge. The average cost of equity funds was 24 per cent of the finance charge or $2.42 per $100, about one-third of which was paid out to stockholders in dividends.

The increase in the average finance charge on consumer credit at commercial banks from 1955 to 1959 was accompanied by a growth in all the major components of cost. Operating expenses increased from $3.76 to $4.17 per $100 of outstanding credit, a rise of 11 per cent. The cost of nonequity funds rose 29 per cent from $1.16 to $1.50 per $100. Although the cost of equity (lender's profit) fluctuated from year to year with no clear trend, the figure for 1959 was higher than that of any of the earlier years covered by the study.

Operating Expenses

Salaries and wages accounted for more than half of the total operating expenses of commercial banks. They averaged $2.33 per $100 of loans in 1959. Individual bank variations in this figure, however, were sizable, ranging between plus and minus 50 per cent of the average. Salary expenses were higher in 1959 than in 1955 but fractionally below 1958 (Chart 8).

Occupancy costs averaged 23 cents per $100 of outstanding credit in 1959. These figures varied relatively little from year to year, ranging from 21 to 23 cents for all years. The amounts allocated for occupancy costs at different banks varied from 12 to 36 cents per $100 of credit.

The advertising figures include all promotional work directly involving the consumer credit department and a share of the bank's over-all public relations and advertising expense. These costs averaged 34 cents per $100 of outstanding credit in 1959, 40 per cent above the 1955 level. Since these costs reflect differences in management policies, the nature of the bank operations, and opinions regarding the desirability and effectiveness of promotional activities, the range among individual institutions was sizable. The highest advertising cost reported for 1959 was more than seven times as large as the lowest.

Provision for losses accounted for 7 per cent of total operating expenses at commercial banks. They averaged 28 cents per $100 of credit in 1959. Actual losses amounted to slightly more than half of this figure in that year. Actual loss fluctuated between 13 and 33 cents per $100 of credit during the five years covered by the study. The highest loss ratio was reported in 1957 when losses exceeded provision for losses by a small amount.

Miscellaneous expenditures amount to about $1.00 per $100 of credit, or 25 per cent of the total operating expenses, and cover a wide variety of expenses that were not classified uniformly by the reporting banks and could not be examined separately. They include credit reports, travel expenses, collection costs, legal fees, office supplies, equipment, and many others.

Cost records maintained by five banks by type of credit reveal substantial differences in costs associated with different types of credit

52

CHART 8

Operating Expenses on Consumer Credit at Commercial Banks, 1955–59
(per $100 of average outstanding credit)

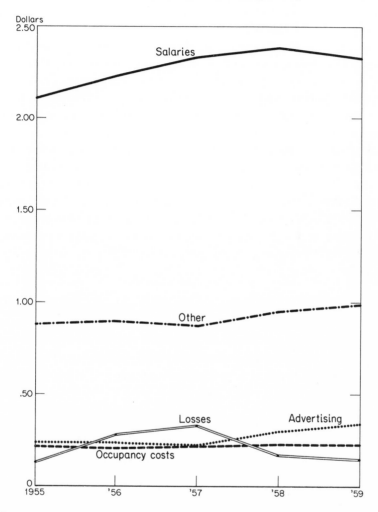

SOURCE: Nine-bank sample. Based on data in Appendix Table D-4.

(Table 17). Operating expenses on appliances and other consumer goods
were more than twice as large as those on automobile paper and substantially above those on personal loans. The variations in costs cannot
be explained completely with information available. Part of difference,
however, arises from number of accounts that must be handled for

every $100 of credit. The outstanding amount of average nonautomotive consumer goods contract was only $220, compared with an average personal loan account of $468 and an average indirect automobile contract of $1,181. The variations in costs by type of credit are discussed in greater detail in Chapter 6.

Individual banks showed a range in their total operating costs from a high of $5.84 to a low of $2.08 per $100 of outstanding credit (Table 16). Banks that concentrated on automobile credit and modernization loans were able to report lower average costs for their entire operation. Banks with large personal loan and appliance operations showed a higher over-all cost.

In contrast to the downward trend in operating expenses at finance companies, bank costs increased from 1955 to 1959. Part of this rise probably reflects the growth in importance of high-cost types of loans. Although bank holdings of nonautomotive consumer goods paper declined in importance, the growth in personal loans more than offset this decline. Personal loans accounted for 28 per cent of their consumer credit in 1959, compared with 17 per cent in 1955.

Nonoperating Expenses

The total cost of funds (both equity and nonequity) and income tax payments was larger than total operating cost at commercial banks accounting for 52 per cent of the gross finance charge in 1959. Slightly more than a fourth of nonoperating expenses, or $1.50 per $100 of outstanding credit, covered the cost of handling time and demand deposits,

TABLE 17

OPERATING EXPENSES AT COMMERCIAL BANKS, BY TYPE OF
CONSUMER CREDIT, 1957–59
(dollars per $100 of average outstanding credit)

Type of Credit	1957	1958	1959
Total consumer credit	3.96	4.14	4.17
Automobile paper, direct	2.73	3.10	2.84
Automobile paper, indirect	2.92	3.03	3.09
Other consumer goods paper	7.43	8.22	7.40
Modernization loans	2.90	3.25	3.49
Personal loans	4.16	4.84	4.36

Source: Totals are based on nine-bank sample. Data by type of loans are based on five-bank subsample.

54

the payment of interest on these deposits and other nonequity funds. The remaining three-fourths represented income taxes and the lender's profit on consumer credit operations.

The cost of funds was 18 per cent higher in 1959 than in 1955 as a result of the higher cost of nonequity funds and higher profits. The cost of nonequity funds grew steadily during this period with the rise in rates paid on time deposits. The cost of equity funds fluctuated from year to year with no perceptible trend. For changes in the relative share of each category of nonoperating expenses, see Chart 9.

CHART 9

Distribution of Nonoperating Expenses on Consumer Credit
at Commercial Banks, 1955–59

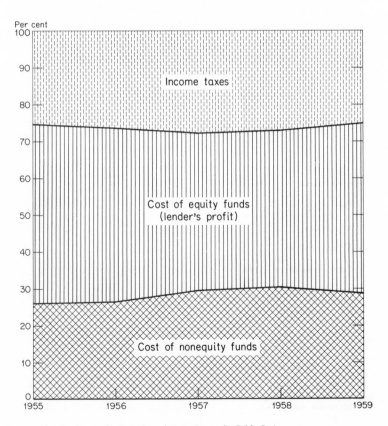

SOURCE: Nine-bank sample. Based on data in Appendix Table D-4.

SOURCES OF FUNDS

Deposits provided nearly 90 per cent of the funds used by commercial banks in 1959. Slightly more than two-thirds of these accounts were in the form of demand deposits with the remainder in savings or time accounts at the end of 1959 (Table 18). The importance of demand deposits varied at individual banks from 46 to 81 per cent. The proportion of demand to time deposits changed relatively little from 1955 through 1959, although the average rate paid on time deposits more than doubled during that period.

Although banks obtain some funds by borrowing from the Federal Reserve System or other banks, the amount of such debt is small. The year-end figures used in the study do not adequately measure the importance of these funds because of the widespread custom of paying down such debts before statement dates.

TABLE 18

SOURCES OF FUNDS FOR COMMERCIAL BANKS, END OF 1959
(per cent)

Item	Mean Distribution	Range of Ratios[a]	
		Maximum	Minimum
Debt	b	b	0
Deposits, total	89.0	92.6	85.8
Demand	61.8	80.8	46.1
Time	27.2	46.5	6.7
Dealer reserves	.2	.5	b
Other liabilities	.9	1.5	.5
Total nonequity funds	90.2	93.4	87.3
Equity funds, total	9.9	12.7	6.6
Reserves	1.9	2.4	.7
Stock and surplus	8.0	10.7	5.5
Total	100.0	--	--

Source: Nine-bank sample.

a
  Components in columns for maximum and minimum ratios are not additive as ratios for individual items were taken from statements of different companies.
  b
  Less than 0.1 per cent.

The sample banks provided an average of 10 per cent of their total resources from equity sources in 1959.[2] The importance of equity funds increased slightly from the end of 1954 to the end of 1959, from 8.4 to 9.9 per cent of total resources, in contrast to the decline in importance of equity funds at finance companies. Individual banks showed a range in the use of equity funds from 6.6 to 12.7 per cent of total resources.

COST OF NONEQUITY FUNDS

The cost of nonequity funds averaged $1.50 per $100 of outstanding consumer credit at the sample commercial banks, or about 15 per cent of the gross finance charge. The costs of these funds reflected the banks' cost of acquiring deposits, the proportion of nonequity funds required for their consumer credit operations, and the proportion of resources held in nonearning forms.

Since interest payments are not permitted on demand deposits, the cost of these funds arises from the servicing of accounts. The total cost is reduced by the service charges paid by the depositors but part of the cost is borne by the bank. Estimates of handling deposits can only be obtained from cost accounting records because of the intermingling of the costs of handling deposits with other bank activities. The methods of allocating costs differed somewhat among the sample banks but all of the banks had made detailed studies of the costs of handling deposits. Estimates of the net costs of handling both time and demand deposits averaged 0.7 per cent of deposits in 1959. In addition, the banks paid an average of 2.7 per cent interest on their time deposits. The combined costs of all nonequity funds, including noninterest-bearing liabilities of various types, was 1.2 per cent in 1959 (Table 19, line 2).

During the period covered by the study, banks increased the rate paid on time deposits from 1.2 to 2.7 per cent. This increase was the principal factor in the rise in the total cost of nonequity funds from .9 to 1.2 per cent, although the costs of handling and servicing deposits rose slightly.

The effective cost of funds used in consumer lending by banks was increased by the cost of funds that had to be held in nonearning forms. Many banks compute the money costs of their lending by subtracting nonearning assets from the amount of nonequity funds in obtaining the effective rate on these funds. The large reserve balances required of

[2] Reserves for losses on loans have been included in equity funds for purposes of this study, although they are usually deducted in computing the value of loans and investments in bank statements.

TABLE 19

COST OF NONEQUITY FUNDS AT COMMERCIAL BANKS, 1955-59
(per cent of average outstanding balances)

Ratio of Dollar Cost of Nonequity Funds to:	1955	1956	1957	1958	1959
Debt and deposits	1.0	1.1	1.2	1.2	1.3
Total nonequity	.9	1.0	1.2	1.2	1.2
Nonequity funds minus nonearning assets	1.3	1.4	1.6	1.6	1.7
Consumer credit receivables[a]	1.2	1.3	1.5	1.5	1.5
Interest on time deposits to average time deposits	1.2	1.6	2.1	2.4	2.7

Source: Nine-bank sample.

[a]Based on the dollar share of the total cost of nonequity funds allocated to consumer credit receivables by the ratio of consumer receivables to total earning assets.

banks and other nonearning assets added about 25 per cent to the effective cost of funds used in their lending. Their total nonequity funds cost them an average of 1.2 per cent in 1959, but after allowance for nonearning assets the effective rate was 1.7 per cent.

Nonequity funds supply about 90 per cent of the funds used in consumer credit. The average cost of these funds per $100 of outstanding credit is, therefore, about 10 per cent less than the effective cost of the funds to the bank. This difference is indicated by the spread between the ratio of the cost of funds to net nonequity funds (Table 19, line 3) and the ratio of the cost of funds to consumer assets (Table 19, line 4).

COST OF EQUITY FUNDS

The cost of equity funds (lender's profit) amounted to 24 per cent of the gross finance charges on consumer credit at commercial banks, or $2.42 per $100 of outstanding credit in 1959. The cost of these funds varied from year to year without any clear trend indicated for the five years studied.

This component of the gross finance charge provides the inducement for banks to extend consumer credit and must be large enough in the long run to justify continuation of consumer lending. The banks in the sample obtained an average of from $2.06 to $2.42 per $100 of outstanding credit on the consumer activities during the five years of the study.

The adequacy of these amounts as return on funds invested can best be examined in the context of all factors affecting bank profits.

Lender's Rate of Profit

The bank's share from consumer credit is only one component of its profits. The sample commercial banks reported a profit on equity funds of 7.6 per cent after taxes in 1959, although they obtained only 2.4 per cent from their consumer lending. Thus they were able to earn 5.2 percentage points more on their equity than they received on the dollars per hundred invested in consumer credit. Their over-all profit on equity also depends upon: the return obtained from other loans and investments; the proportion of their total resources they invest in earning assets; and the financial advantages of the use of nonequity funds. The relative importance of these items in bank profits are illustrated in Table 20.

RETURN ON OTHER EARNING ASSETS

Banks invest in a wide range of loans and investments. Some of these investments may produce a higher net operating income than consumer credit, others a smaller income. The sample banks reported a net operating income on all earning assets of 3.4 per cent in 1959 (Table 20, line 2) as opposed to 5.3 per cent on consumer credit.

The relatively low return on some of their nonconsumer credit activities is related to the deposit function of banks. They are required to seek investment outlets that are liquid and of good quality to protect their depositors and provide the liquidity needed to service demand deposits. The low yield on such investments reduces their earning capacity and is a cost of accepting deposits.

In most cases the loan and investment decisions of commercial banks are not influenced directly by their consumer credit policies. However, some banks find it desirable to finance the inventory of the dealers from which they obtain retail paper or in other ways provide services related to consumer lending. In some states banks are permitted to handle insurance operations or to accept fees as agents for writing insurance. In such cases, the insurance that arises from consumer credit operations may add to or supplement the bank's income. Most of their earnings on other earning assets, however, have no relation to their consumer credit activities.

TABLE 20

FACTORS IN COMMERCIAL BANK PROFITS, 1955–59
(per cent of average outstanding balances)

Ratio	1955	1956	1957	1958	1959
1. Net operating income from consumer credit to consumer receivables[a]	4.5	4.9	5.0	4.9	5.3
2. Net operating income to earning assets	2.3	2.9	3.3	3.4	3.4
3. Net operating income to total assets	1.9	2.1	2.4	2.5	2.5
4. Profits before taxes to equity funds	12.5	13.6	14.8	15.5	14.5
5. Net return from nonequity to equity funds (line 4 minus line 3)	10.6	11.5	12.4	13.0	12.0
6. Provision for income taxes to profit before taxes	46.8	46.6	49.5	48.9	46.0
7. Net profits to equity funds	6.5	7.1	7.4	7.9	7.6
8. Percentage of profit obtained from leverage on nonequity funds (line 5 ÷ line 4)	84.8	84.6	83.8	83.9	82.7
ALTERNATIVE DERIVATION OF LINE 5					
a. Net operating income to total assets (line 3) _less_	1.9	2.1	2.4	2.5	2.5
b. Cost of nonequity funds to nonequity funds _equals_	.9	1.0	1.2	1.2	1.2
c. Net return from nonequity funds to nonequity funds _times_	1.0	1.1	1.2	1.3	1.3
d. Leverage coefficient (ratio of nonequity to equity funds) _equals_	11.0	10.5	10.1	9.9	9.6
e. Net return from nonequity to equity funds (line 5)[b]	11.0	11.6	12.1	12.9	12.5

a
  Equivalent to nonoperating expenses per $100 of average outstanding consumer credit, see Table 16.
  b
  Differences between lines 5 and e result from rounding errors introduced by alternative methods of calculation.

COST OF NONEARNING ASSETS

Banks are required to hold a sizable part of their total resources in the form of reserves because of their unique responsibility to their depositors and their key role in the determination of the money supply. As a result, a large share of their total resources are immobilized for earning purposes. In 1959, 24.5 per cent of their resources were held in the form of cash, bank balances, or reserves with the Federal Reserve System. Another 1.5 per cent was held in other nonearning assets. These large idle balances reduce the earning potential and profitability of banking operations. Their net operating income of 3.4 per cent on earning assets produced a return of only 2.5 per cent on total resources in 1959 (Table 20, line 3).

The return of 2.5 per cent that banks earned on total resources is obviously too small to attract or hold equity funds. A satisfactory return can only be achieved by the sizable financial advantage that banks obtain on the use of deposit funds. The importance of this advantage depends on the cost of these funds and the proportion of total resources obtained from nonequity sources.

Banks obtained their total nonequity funds at an average rate of 1.2 per cent in 1959 and earned an average of 2.5 per cent on total resources. Thus they were able to net about 1.3 per cent on all the nonequity funds used. Their nonequity funds were 9.6 times larger than their net worth so that the return on equity from the use of nonequity funds was 9.6 times 1.3 per cent, or about 12.5 per cent (see lower panel of Table 20). This income, plus the return that could be earned directly on the owner's share of total resources resulted in a net profit before taxes of 14.5 per cent on equity funds. Provisions for income taxes absorbed 46 per cent of the profits before taxes leaving a return of about 7.6 per cent on equity in 1959.

The ratio of net profits to equity funds at the sample banks increased steadily during the five years covered by the study. The improvement in profits reflected primarily an increase in net operating income as the sample banks were able to increase their net operating income on total assets by nearly a third. This income was more than enough to offset the increase in cost of nonequity funds and the decline in the ratio of nonequity funds to total resources.

Income from consumer credit added to the increase in earnings on total assets. Their net operating income from consumer credit rose from 4.5 to 5.3 per cent. Their net income from all earning assets rose by nearly a half, from 2.3 to 3.4 per cent. The increase in interest rates during the 1950's contributed materially to high earning rates at banks and was more than enough to offset the higher cost of their funds.

The sample banks used about half of their profits for cash dividends to shareholders and retained the rest. In 1959 they paid dividends amounting to two-thirds of their profits. These payments gave the stockholders an average yield of about 5 per cent on the book value of their stock, compared to 1955 when the sample banks paid out only 55 per cent of their profits for an average yield of only 3.6 per cent on the book value of their stock.

Comparison of Banks with Highest and Lowest Average Finance Charges

Two banks in the sample consistently showed high finance charges on consumer credit throughout the period covered; two others showed consistently low charges. The finance charges at the high-charge banks averaged $3.90 per $100 higher than those at the low-charge banks for the five-year period.

No clear-cut difference in the type of loans made by the banks involved could be found. They all performed a wide range of consumer lending operations. All but one of them had both direct and indirect automobile lending operations and some indirect paper on other consumer durable goods. All of them had about the same proportion of their receivables in personal loans and all but one had 10 to 15 per cent of their receivables in modernization loans.

The high-charge banks showed somewhat higher expenses in every item of operating expenses on consumer activities except advertising. They also reported 25 per cent higher costs on nonequity funds. The difference in cost of nonequity funds reflected primarily a greater dependence on time deposits by the high-charge banks. They obtained 30 per cent of their total resources from time deposits, compared with 10 per cent at the low-charge group.

Only 23 per cent of the differential in finance charges could be traced to operating expenses and the cost of nonequity funds. The remaining 77 per cent was in the return on equity funds and provisions for income taxes. The high-charge banks earned an average of 8.4 per cent on their net worth, compared with only 5.5 per cent at the low-charge banks.

The profits of high-charge banks could not be attributed solely to their favorable earnings on consumer credit, however. They also showed a higher return on their other earning assets, more complete utilization of the resources, and greater leverage than the low-charge banks (Table 21).

TABLE 21

COMPARISON OF COMMERCIAL BANKS WITH HIGHEST AND LOWEST
AVERAGE FINANCE CHARGES ON CONSUMER CREDIT, 1955-59[a]

Item	Two High-Charge Banks (1)	Two Low-Charge Banks (2)	Difference (col. 1 minus col. 2) (3)
DOLLARS PER $100 OF AVERAGE OUTSTANDING CONSUMER CREDIT			
Finance charges[b]	10.90	7.00	3.90
Operating expenses	3.80	3.40	.40
Salaries	2.20	2.00	.20
Occupancy costs	.30	.10	.20
Advertising	.20	.40	-.20
Provision for losses	.30	.20	.10
Actual losses	(.3)	(.2)	(.1)
Other	.80	.70	.10
Nonoperating expenses (lender's net operating income)	7.10	3.60	3.50
Cost of nonequity funds	1.90	1.40	.50
Income tax	1.70	.70	1.00
Cost of equity funds (lender's profit)	3.50	1.50	1.00
Dividends	2.50	1.10	1.40
Retained	1.00	.40	.60
SELECTED RATIOS (PER CENT)			
Total net operating income to earning assets	3.5	2.7	.8
Total net operating income to total assets	2.8	2.0	.8
Cost of nonequity funds to nonequity funds	1.6	1.2	.4
Nonequity to equity funds	12.6	8.5	4.1
Time deposit to total assets	30.0	10.0	20.0
Net profits to equity funds	8.4	5.5	2.9

[a]
All data are averages of individual bank ratios for the five
years 1955-59.
[b]
Excludes dealer's share of gross finance charges.

CHAPTER 5

Federal Credit Unions

CREDIT unions differ from the other institutions covered in this study because they are consumer cooperatives with the dual objective of encouraging savings and providing credit for their members. Their lending operations are restricted to their membership, which is typically limited to definable groups with some common affiliation, such as the employees of a business concern, government agency, or the members of a church or fraternal group.

The cooperative nature of credit unions plays an important role in determining the level of their gross finance charges. Their operations are subsidized in part by the voluntary work of their members and by direct or indirect assistance from sponsoring organizations. They obtain most of their funds from their membership in the form of savings and do not have to provide the return required for risk capital obtained from equity markets. As cooperatives, they are exempt from income taxes levied on other financial institutions.

Federal credit unions operate under federal charters and supervision, which prescribe in considerable detail the nature of their operations and requires annual examinations by federal authorities. Maximum charges on loans are set at 1 per cent a month on the unpaid balance and the maximum maturity is five years. Unsecured loans are limited in size to $750 and the maximum loan of any kind is limited to 10 per cent of the organization's paid-in capital and surplus. Other sections of the law specify the organization of individual credit unions and outline many of the details of their operations.

Individual credit unions are similar in many respects because of the centralized control and supervision, but they differ widely in size and administration. They vary from the small credit union with a few thousand dollars in assets, part-time management, and no regular hours or office space to the multimillion dollar credit union with professional management and full-time operations.

The information used in this study is based on compilations prepared for all federal credit unions by the Bureau of Federal Credit Unions. Financial ratios were computed from aggregate data and are, therefore, weighted by the dollar amounts at individual credit unions rather than by a unit weight for each company as in other parts of the study. The distribution of federal credit unions by asset size as shown in Table 22 indicates the relative importance of different size groups in the total.

TABLE 22

NUMBER AND DISTRIBUTION OF FEDERAL CREDIT UNIONS
BY ASSET SIZE, END OF 1959

Asset Size (dollars)	Number	Total Assets	
		Thousand Dollars	Per Cent
Total	9,447	2,352,813	100.0
Under 5,000	637	1,563	.1
5,000 to 9,999	563	4,146	.2
10,000 to 24,999	1,188	20,222	.9
25,000 to 49,999	1,342	49,212	2.1
50,000 to 99,999	1,506	108,843	4.6
100,000 to 249,999	1,989	321,760	13.7
250,000 to 499,999	1,084	385,087	16.4
500,000 to 999,999	653	448,747	19.0
1,000,000 to 1,999,999	337	456,615	19.4
2,000,000 to 4,999,999	122	348,701	14.8
5,000,000 and over	26	207,917	8.8

Source: 1959 Report of Operations, Federal Credit Unions,
U.S. Department of Health, Education, and Welfare, Table 14,
p. 20.

Appendix A contains a detailed description of the processing of the federal credit union data used in this study.

Uses of Funds

Federal credit unions are limited in their use of funds to loans to their members or to other credit unions, investments in U. S. government securities, and deposits in banks or savings and loan associations. At the end of 1959, 70 per cent of their assets were in loans to members (Table 23). They make personal cash loans for purchases of household goods, consolidation of debt, payment of insurance, hospital, or medical expenses, or any other personal needs. Most of their loans are small, except those for the purchase of automobiles which accounted for 30 per cent of the dollar amount and 13 per cent of the number of loans made in 1956.[1] Their automobile loans are similar in nature to other cash loans except that they are usually larger in amount and are secured by

[1] *1956 Report of Operations, Federal Credit Unions,* U. S. Department of Health, Education, and Welfare, p. 12.

TABLE 23

USES OF FUNDS BY FEDERAL CREDIT UNIONS, END OF 1959
(per cent)

		Asset Size (dollars)		
Item	All Asset Sizes	1,000,000 and Over	50,000 to 999,999	Under 50,000
Earning assets	93.1	94.0	92.8	86.1
Consumer loans	70.8	68.3	72.6	75.3
Other	22.3	25.7	20.2	10.8
Cash and bank balances	5.9	4.6	6.4	13.1
Other assets	1.0	1.4	.8	.8
Total	100.0	100.0	100.0	100.0

Source: Based on data published by the Bureau of Federal Credit Unions.

the automobile. They frequently carry the same finance charges as other loans.

Since credit unions can only make loans to members, they frequently have more funds than they need to satisfy the loan demand. Excess funds may be invested in government securities or in savings and loan shares. Investments of this type accounted for 22 per cent of the total assets of all federal credit unions in 1959.

The availability of funds for investment in assets other than loans varies greatly at different credit unions. Some have a loan demand in excess of the savings they attract; others have to limit the saving they accept or invest a sizable proportion of their funds at low yields. The older and larger credit unions usually have a larger share of their funds in government securities or saving and loan shares than the newer organizations. Larger credit unions—those with assets of more than $1 million—had 26 per cent of their assets in such investments in 1959 while those with assets of less than $50,000 had only 11 per cent in non-consumer investments (Table 23). A similar difference appears between the portfolios of well-established and new credit unions. Credit unions in existence twenty-five years carried ten times as much of their assets in government securities and savings and loan shares as those in existence less than a year.[2]

[2] 1959 Report of Operations, Federal Credit Unions, p. 13.

Every credit union must hold some of its funds in cash and demand accounts to meet its operating needs. Since they are not subject to reserve requirements or to demands from creditors for compensating balances, the amount of cash they hold depends upon their operating needs and the alertness of their managers in converting idle balances into earning assets. The ratio of cash balances to total assets declines with the age and size of the credit union. New credit unions hold a considerably larger share of their assets in cash and bank balances, while older ones, either because of experience or more predictable liquidity requirements, invest a larger share of their funds. The larger credit unions held less than 5 per cent of assets in cash, while the small ones averaged 13 per cent.

Finance Charges

Finance charges at federal credit unions average $10.04 per $100 of outstanding loans for 1959. The actual cost of credit to consumers was somewhat smaller, however, because life insurance is often covered by the charge and partial interest refunds may be made. Interest refunds were first authorized in 1954 by an amendment to the Federal Credit Union Act. After the cost of credit life insurance and the value of refunds is deducted, the adjusted finance charge averaged $9.13 per $100 of loans in 1959.

Finance charges of individual credit unions varied as did practices with respect to interest refunds and free life insurance. The average adjusted finance charge was slightly less than 9 per cent at the credit unions with more than $1 million in assets and somewhat more than 9 per cent at the smaller credit unions; 17 per cent of all federal credit unions refunded some interest, while 89 per cent provided borrowers' life insurance.[3] Interest refunds were larger at the million-dollar credit unions, but a larger proportion of the small organizations refunded interest.

Finance charges at credit unions have not changed greatly in the past two decades. They averaged $10.88 per $100 of outstanding credit in 1939, as opposed to $10.04 per $100 in 1959. The net cost to consumers has probably declined, however, with the growth of interest refunds and free insurance. Separate data are not available in earlier years to adjust gross figures to obtain estimates of the actual finance charge, but before World War II interest refunds were not permitted and credit life insur-

[3] *Ibid.,* p. 10.

ance was less commonly used. The adjusted finance charge in 1959 of $9.13 per $100 of loans was 16 per cent below the unadjusted finance charge in 1939. A substantial part of this difference represents a decline in average cost of credit to the consumer.

Components of Finance Charges

Credit union operations involve most of the costs incurred by private lenders. The difference lies primarily in the extent of free services available to credit unions from their membership or sponsors. They incur costs in extending credit, maintaining records, and collecting loans. In addition, they must pay for the funds used in making loans. Since most of their funds come from their members, they must pay enough in the form of cash dividends or service to attract the savings of their members.

Credit unions are difficult to compare with stockholder-owned institutions because the shareholders play a dual role of depositor and stockholder. The cash dividends paid to shareholders are similar to the dividends paid to stockholders, while funds retained in the credit union increase the shareholder's net worth just as in a stockholder-owned company. The shareholders in a credit union may receive free life insurance in addition to many of the benefits of the depositors of a bank or savings institution. In a private institution the cost of handling deposits is a cost of obtaining the nonequity funds. In a credit union the depositors (shareholders) and owners are the same people and the funds they provide could be regarded as nonequity or equity funds. Similarly, the payments to shareholders and the costs of handling their accounts could be regarded as either a cost of nonequity or equity funds. If they were treated as a cost of nonequity funds, they would be deducted in arriving at net income. For purposes of this study, the costs of handling share accounts were treated as a service rendered to the shareholders and considered part of the cost of equity funds.[4] The cost of handling shares had to be estimated, as no separate cost data were available. These estimates were necessarily rather crude but they indicate the approximate magnitude of an essential element in the cost of credit union operations. The estimates were based on the analogous operations of banks with respect to time deposits with allowances for the lower operating costs of credit unions.

The return on equity funds represents the largest component of the finance charge at credit unions and in 1959 accounted for 63 per cent

[4] For a similar treatment of payments to shareholders as a cost of equity, see John T. Croteau, *The Federal Credit Unions,* New York, 1956, p. 91.

of adjusted charges (Table 24). Operating expenses, including salaries and wages, rent, supplies, and losses on loans, accounted for 36 per cent and the cost of borrowed funds for only 1 per cent of the total.

No clear trend in the major components of credit union costs is evident from the data for 1949–59. Year-to-year fluctuations were larger than the changes that took place over the period covered by the study.

Operating Expenses

The operating expenses of credit unions are not fully covered by the dollar costs reported in their accounting statements. A substantial share of their costs is absorbed by voluntary services from members or by the provision of office space or other assistance by sponsoring organizations, and no estimate is possible of the dollar value of these contributions. A rough indication of the costs of providing similar services under less advantageous conditions can be obtained, however, by comparing their

TABLE 24

COMPONENTS OF FINANCE CHARGES ON CONSUMER CREDIT AT FEDERAL CREDIT UNIONS, 1959
(per $100 of average outstanding credit)

Item	Distribution	
	Dollars	Per Cent
Adjusted finance charges (lender's gross revenue)[a]	9.13	100.0
Operating expenses	3.30	36.1
Salaries	1.77	19.3
Occupancy costs	.06	.6
Advertising	.07	.8
Losses charged off	.38	4.2
Other	1.02	11.2
Nonoperating expenses	5.83	63.9
Cost of nonequity	.12	1.3
Cost of equity funds	5.71	62.6
Retained	.98	10.7
Service to shareholders[b]	.73	8.0
Dividends	4.00	43.9

Source: Based on data published by the Bureau of Federal Credit Unions.
  a
  Includes all finance charges and fees collected on loans. The cost of free insurance provided borrowers and interest refunds were deducted.
  b
  Includes cost of free life insurance for shareholders and cost of handling share accounts.

69

operating expenses with those of consumer finance companies. The operating expenses of the nine-company sample of consumer finance companies averaged $14.25 per $100 of outstanding loans in 1959, compared with $3.30 per $100 reported by the federal credit unions.

Most of the operating expenses of credit unions are similar to those of other credit grantors. Loans must be screened and investigated; records must be maintained; payments must be made and loans collected. The size and value of many of these costs are very different for a cooperative organization with a limited field of membership than for a stockholder-owned organization operating with the public. Credit investigations and collections are handled in different ways and advertising and promotion expenses are much less important.

Salaries comprise the largest item of credit union operating expenses and averaged 54 per cent of the total in 1959 (Table 24). League dues and supervisory fees accounted for 9 per cent of total operating expenses, while rent and other occupancy costs amounted to only 2 per cent.

The pattern of expenses varied widely with the size of the credit union. Salary costs tend to increase with the size of the organization; they accounted for 63 per cent of the adjusted expenses of credit unions with assets of at least $1 million, but only 46 per cent of the expenses of those with assets of less than $50,000 in 1959.[5] As credit unions grow and expand in size, voluntary help becomes inadequate to meet operating needs and more full-time and professional help is needed.

Despite the growth in salary cost with the size of operations, total expenses in relation to income tend to decline with the age of the organization. Data published by the Bureau of Federal Credit Unions show considerably higher ratios of expenses to income for credit unions in operation eight years or less than for those in operation twenty years or more.[6] This suggests that rising age implies a growth in managerial experience and efficiency which, when combined with the advantages of size, more than offsets the increase in salary costs associated with increasing size.

Total operating expenses per $100 of outstanding loans declined slightly from 1949 to 1959, which reflected a drop in average salary expenditures per $100 of loans. All other cost items were slightly higher. Available data are not adequate to explain fully the decline in salary expenses. The growth in the average size of loan from $260 in 1949 to

---

[5] *1959 Report of Operations, Federal Credit Unions*, p. 25. Published figures for total expenses were adjusted to exclude interest on borrowed money and expenses of borrowers' and life savings insurance.

[6] *Ibid.*, p. 14.

$593 in 1959 undoubtedly helped reduce the costs per dollar. The increased efficiency and management experience that accompany the aging of credit unions may also have played a part. The share of average salary cost in operating expenses at all federal credit unions between 1949 and 1959 dropped from 60 to 54 per cent.

Losses charged off in any year depend in part upon economic conditions, so that trends are difficult to detect over such a short period. Loan losses per $100 of loans were higher on an average in the last half of the 1950's than in the first half, although the highest loss rate was recorded in the postrecession year of 1954.

Sources of Funds

Federal credit unions depend mostly upon the savings of their members for their loanable funds. Almost 90 per cent of their resources were derived from shares of members at the end of 1959. The proportion varied somewhat with the size and age of the credit union, and was higher at the older and larger credit unions than at the younger and smaller organizations (Table 25).

TABLE 25

SOURCES OF FUNDS FOR FEDERAL CREDIT UNIONS, END OF 1959
(per cent)

Item	All Asset Sizes	Asset Size (dollars)		
		1,000,000 and Over	50,000 to 999,999	Under 50,000
Debt	2.5	1.8	3.0	4.0
Other liabilities	0.5	0.7	0.3	0.3
Total nonequity funds	3.0	2.5	3.3	4.3
Shares	88.2	88.7	87.8	87.9
Reserves and undivided earnings	8.8	8.8	8.9	7.8
Total equity funds	97.0	97.5	96.7	95.7
Total	100.0	100.0	100.0	100.0

Source: Based on data published by the Bureau of Federal Credit Unions.

Borrowing plays a minor role in most credit union operations. Smaller credit unions—those with assets of less than $50,000—obtained 4 per cent of their total resources by borrowing in 1959. The average for all credit unions was only 2.5 per cent. Many of them are faced with the problem of finding outlets for surplus funds rather than with a shortage of funds.

Reserves and undistributed earnings provided an average of 9 per cent of the total credit unions' funds in 1959. Most of this amount was in reserves of various types. The Federal Credit Union Law requires that 20 per cent of earnings must be set aside for a regular reserve until the amount of the reserves reaches 10 per cent of shares. In addition, it requires that a special reserve be established to cover questionable loans when the regular reserve has not reached full size. The size of the special reserve is determined by the amount and the age of delinquent loans.

Nonoperating Expenses

The nonoperating costs of federal credit unions averaged $5.83 per $100 of outstanding loans, or 64 per cent of the adjusted finance charge in 1959 (Table 24). Since credit unions do not pay income taxes and use relatively small amounts of nonequity funds, nearly all of this amount represents the cost of equity funds. Half of the finance charge was paid to shareholders either in cash dividends or services of various types; 10 per cent was retained in reserves and undistributed earnings.

Nonequity funds play such a small role in credit union operations that the costs of these funds represented about 1 per cent of the finance charge, or 12 cents per $100 of outstanding loans. Although the rate paid for borrowed funds by federal credit unions has increased since 1949, the increase has been smaller than the rise in market rates in general. The cost of interest on borrowed funds as a percentage of total nonequity funds rose from 2.4 to 3.8 per cent. Credit unions were able to offset the increase in the cost of funds by more efficient use of their resources. The percentage of total assets held in cash, bank balances, and other non-earning forms declined from 11 to 8 per cent during the same period. The net cost of nonequity funds used in their lending operations accordingly changed very little.

Net Income

All borrowers from credit unions must also be shareholders. In practice, however, the membership of a credit union can be divided into two fairly distinct groups: those who are predominantly savers and those who are predominantly borrowers. The dual objective of the credit union movement requires that both groups be considered in management decisions. Each credit union, however, has considerable flexibility within the range of market competition to adjust the flow of funds between the borrower and saver groups. Earnings can be distributed in dividends to shareholders or, since 1954, as interest refunds to borrowers. The rates on loans may be adjusted, within legal limits, to increase or decrease the earnings available for dividends. The dividends paid on shares together with the services available to the shareholders must be large enough to attract and hold funds in the organization and the rate on loans must be low enough to meet competition. Within these limits, however, the management can pursue a variety of policies and objectives designed to accommodate both borrowers and savers.

As a result of the dual objective of credit union management, the attempt to maximize the return on equity funds probably does not play as important a role in credit union decisions as in those of stockholder-owned companies. The demands of the credit union shareholders must be met, however, because they provide the bulk of the funds and in many cases dominate the management. Cash dividends and services must be enough to attract and hold their savings, and the total return must be large enough to build the required reserves.

The return on equity funds (net income to equity funds) at credit unions averaged about 5 per cent from 1949 to 1959, including the cost of handling share accounts and the cost of life insurance for shareholders (Table 28). Cash dividends in 1959 were only 3.4 per cent of equity and fell below 3 per cent in a number of years. This relatively low return on equity compared with net earnings of between 5 and 6 per cent on consumer lending activities reflects the low yield on nonconsumer investments, the cost of nonearning assets, and the minor importance of the use of borrowed funds.

RETURN ON OTHER EARNING ASSETS

The return from other earning assets of credit unions reduces the effective return on their consumer credit. Since they are only permitted to invest in government securities, savings and loan shares, or loans to other credit unions, the yield on the other earning assets is low. In 1959 these earnings were 3.8 per cent of invested funds, compared with 9.1 per cent on consumer loans (Table 26).

The return on nonconsumer investments improved slightly during the period with the rise in interest rates. Credit unions earned an average

73

TABLE 26

SELECTED EARNING RATIOS FOR FEDERAL CREDIT UNIONS, 1949-59
(per cent)

Year	Ratio of Earnings to Invested Funds		Ratio of Net Operating Income to Invested Funds		
	Consumer Loans	Other Earning Assets	Consumer Loans	All Earning Assets	Total Assets
1949	9.4	2.9	5.9	4.8	4.3
1950	9.7	2.9	6.5	5.4	4.8
1951	9.6	2.7	6.1	5.1	4.5
1952	9.5	3.0	6.1	5.2	4.6
1953	9.7	3.1	6.4	5.5	4.9
1954	9.6	3.1	6.0	5.3	4.7
1955	9.6	3.1	6.6	5.7	5.1
1956	9.5	3.2	6.3	5.5	5.0
1957	9.3	3.5	6.1	5.5	4.9
1958	9.2	3.5	5.9	5.3	4.8
1959	9.1	3.8	5.8	5.3	4.9

Source: Based on data published by the Bureau of Federal Credit Unions.

of 3.8 per cent on their nonconsumer assets in 1959, compared with 2.9 per cent in 1949. This was still well below the net operating income that they made on consumer assets, however.

Nonearning assets reduced the return on total funds employed so that credit unions averaged 4.9 per cent on their total assets, compared with a return of 5.3 per cent on their invested funds in 1959. Over the eleven years studied, credit unions reduced the proportion of assets held in nonearning forms and narrowed the spread between the rate earned on invested funds and that earned on all funds.

RETURN FROM NONEQUITY FUNDS

Borrowed funds add relatively little to the return of credit unions because the amounts involved are so small. Since credit unions only obtain, on an average, 2-3 per cent of their funds from nonequity sources, the financial advantage or leverage obtained from these funds is not very important to the net income of credit unions. Table 27 shows the contribution of nonequity funds to the return of net worth of credit unions, which is only a fraction of a percentage point. Credit unions have very little of the financial advantage of using borrowed funds that is so important in the operations of stockholder-owned institutions. The rate

TABLE 27

RETURN FROM USE OF NONEQUITY FUNDS AT FEDERAL CREDIT UNIONS, 1949-59
(per cent)

Year	Ratio of Net Operating Income to Total Assets (1)	Ratio of Cost of Nonequity Funds to Nonequity Funds (2)	Ratio of Net Return on Nonequity Funds to Nonequity Funds[a] (3)	Ratio of Nonequity Funds to Equity (4)	Ratio of Net Return from Nonequity Funds to Equity Funds[b] (5)
1949	4.3	2.2	2.1	.0295	.06
1950	4.8	2.9	1.9	.0342	.06
1951	4.5	2.8	1.7	.0273	.04
1952	4.6	2.9	1.7	.0243	.04
1953	4.9	3.1	1.8	.0282	.05
1954	4.7	3.0	1.7	.0251	.04
1955	5.1	3.2	1.9	.0246	.05
1956	5.0	3.2	1.8	.0263	.05
1957	5.0	3.6	1.4	.0264	.04
1958	4.8	3.3	1.6	.0244	.04
1959	4.9	3.1	1.8	.0269	.05

Source: Based on data published by the Bureau of Federal Credit Unions.

[a] Column 1 minus column 2.

[b] Column 3 times column 4.

earned by credit unions on their assets is very close to the rate they earn on net worth.

Disposition of Net Income

The net income of credit unions, which is the counterpart of net profits at the other type of institution, ranged between 4.3 and 5.2 per cent of total assets during the eleven years covered by the study (Table 28). The return fluctuated from year to year with no distinct trend. The proportion of net income paid in cash dividends increased from 63 per cent in 1949 to nearly 70 per cent in 1959.

The net income figures used in this study include the costs of services rendered to the shareholders—the cost of handling share accounts and the cost of life insurance. The value of these services increased slightly during the 1950's, and in 1959 they accounted for 14 per cent of net income.

The value of combined benefits to shareholders accounted for 83 per cent of net income in 1959, compared to 75 per cent in 1949. The

TABLE 28

NET INCOME AND DIVIDENDS AT FEDERAL CREDIT UNIONS, 1949–59
(per cent)

Year	Net Income as Percentage of Equity Funds	Disposition of Net Income				Dividends as Percentage of Shares
		Total	Retained	Services to Shareholders[a]	Dividends	
1949	4.3	100.0	24.8	12.4	62.8	2.9
1950	4.9	100.0	29.4	10.6	60.0	3.1
1951	4.6	100.0	24.0	13.4	62.6	3.1
1952	4.6	100.0	23.0	13.5	63.5	3.2
1953	5.0	100.0	26.1	12.5	61.4	3.3
1954	4.8	100.0	22.3	13.1	64.5	3.4
1955	5.2	100.0	22.7	12.3	61.0	3.4
1956	5.1	100.0	22.3	12.8	64.9	3.6
1957	5.1	100.0	20.9	13.0	66.1	3.7
1958	4.9	100.0	16.8	14.0	69.2	3.7
1959	5.0	100.0	16.9	13.9	69.2	3.8

Source: Based on data published by the Bureau of Federal Credit Unions.

[a]Includes cost of life insurance for shareholders and estimate of cost of handling share accounts.

increase in importance of dividends and other direct benefits resulted in a drop in the proportion of net income retained in reserves and undistributed earnings. This decline probably reflects in large part the attainment of the level of reserves specified by the Federal Credit Union Law by many of the credit unions. After the required level is reached, a share of net income no longer has to be allocated to reserves, and a larger proportion can be devoted to dividends. There is very little incentive for most credit unions to retain earnings because they frequently have to place any excess funds in low-yielding investments that reduce the average return on assets.

Dividend payments in 1959 amounted to 3.8 per cent of the value of average outstanding shares, which compares with a rate of 2.9 per cent in 1949 and follows the general rise in savings rates that took place during that period at all savings institutions. Actual dividend payments differ widely at individual credit unions. About 6 per cent of the federal credit unions paid 6 per cent on their shares in 1959, while 3 per cent paid less than 3 per cent. The median rate was 4.4 per cent.[7]

[7] *Ibid.*, p. 7.

CHAPTER 6

Comparison of Cost of Providing Consumer Credit at Four Types of Financial Institutions

THE variation in average finance charges on consumer credit among institutional groups is impressive.[1] Average annual charges in 1959 varied from $9 to $24 per $100 of credit outstanding among the four types of institutions studied (Table 29). Averages for individual companies showed a range from $7 to $31 per $100. These differences reflect many variations in amount and type of credit extended as well as alternative cost factors faced by different institutions.

A substantial part of these differences can be traced to the handling and operating costs of the type of lending performed by the institutions. The lender's decisions on the maturity, size, and type of loan to be made, as well as the character of the credit risk he assumes, determine the general level of his costs. His individual operating procedures and efficiency establish his own particular pattern of costs.

Other differences in charges stem from the legal, tax, and institutional framework within which the lender operates, and are of special interest because they determine the ability of lenders to compete in similar markets and because they have implications about the economic effects of legislative action. Perhaps the sharpest difference among the institutions studied occurs between the federal credit unions and the other three types. Credit unions are owned by the users (borrowers and savers), while the other types of institutions are owned by stockholders.

Table 29 gives a breakdown of the expenses of providing credit at each type of institution and indicates the importance of each cost component in the gross finance charge. Annual operating expenses, which include all the day-to-day costs of handling accounts, ranged from $3.30 per $100 of credit outstanding to nearly five times that amount, or $14.25 per $100. The cost of money varied from $3.92 to $6.89 per $100, and the costs of income taxes varied from zero to $2.73 per $100.

The distribution of costs also varied widely. Operating expenses and payments to dealers accounted for from 48 to 64 per cent of total finance charge at the three types of stockholder-owned institutions. The cost of nonequity funds, provisions for income taxes, and profit made up the remainder. With the exception of credit unions, the cost of funds (interest and profit) was not the major element in total cost to the consumer; it was 29 per cent of the cost for consumer finance and for sales

[1] See note a, Table 29.

77

TABLE 29

COMPONENTS OF GROSS FINANCE CHARGES ON CONSUMER CREDIT,
BY TYPE OF LENDER, 1959
(dollars per $100 of average outstanding credit)

Item	Stockholder-Owned Institutions			All Federal Credit Unions
	Nine Consumer Finance Companies	Ten Sales Finance Companies	Nine Commercial Banks	
Gross finance charges[a]	24.04	16.59	10.04	9.13
Dealer's share of gross finance charges[b]	.17	2.95	.62	0
Lender's gross revenue	23.87	13.64	9.42	9.13
Operating expenses	14.25	7.74	4.17	3.30
Salaries	6.45	3.47	2.33	1.77
Occupancy costs	1.09	.43	.23	.06
Advertising	.89	.31	.34	.07
Provision for losses	1.98	1.46	.28	n.a.
Actual losses[c]	(1.70)	(1.11)	(.15)	.38
Other[d]	3.84	2.07	.99	1.02
Nonoperating expenses	9.62	5.90	5.25	5.83
Cost of nonequity funds	3.97	4.02	1.50	.12
Income taxes	2.73	1.07	1.33	0
Cost of equity funds (lender's profit or net income)[e]	2.92	.81	2.42	5.71
Dividends	2.31	.48	1.49	4.00
Retained	.61	.33	.93	.98
Services to owners[f]	--	--	--	.73

Source: Data for all types except federal credit unions are based on
averages of individual company ratios. Ratios for federal credit unions are
based on tabulations for all federal credit unions.

[a]Includes all finance charges and fees collected on consumer credit activities. Charges for insurance are not included and the cost of free insurance
provided to the borrower was deducted from the gross finance charge.

[b]Represents the estimated difference between the gross finance charges and
the charges which accrue to the financial institution that purchases the credit
contract. The estimates of the dealer's share are based on data from four large
sales finance companies on new- and used-automobile contracts. No quantitative
information was available for estimates of the dealer's share on nonautomotive
contracts, hence no estimate of this was included. This share is known to be
considerably less important than that on automobile contracts and in some cases
the dealer does not receive a share of the charge.

[c]Net of recoveries.

[d]Includes a wide variety of expenses such as travel, office supplies, legal
fees, etc., that could not be obtained on a separate and uniform basis from all
the sample companies.

[e]Because of differences in ownership and objectives, the term net profit is
usually not used for credit unions. The term net income has been used instead.

[f]Includes estimate of cost of servicing share accounts and cost of free life
insurance provided shareholders.

finance companies, 39 per cent for commercial banks, and 64 per cent for credit unions. That is to say, 71 cents of the consumer's cost-of-credit dollar go for expenses other than the cost of money in the case of consumer finance and sales finance companies, 61 cents in the case of banks, and 36 cents in the case of credit unions. The cost of equity (lender's profit) came to 5 per cent of the total for sales finance companies, 12 per cent for consumer finance companies, 24 per cent for banks, and 63 per cent for credit unions. These results depend considerably, as is brought out below, on the relative amounts of equity funds used by the different types of lender.

Variations in Operating Expenses

Comparison of the operating expenses for each type of company (Table 29) indicates that variations in these expenses account for the largest part of the differences in gross finance charges among the four types of institutions. A number of factors can be identified that contribute substantially to differences in operating costs among lenders: (1) the method of acquiring business, whether directly from the public or indirectly through dealers; (2) the character of the risks assumed; (3) the average size of contract; and (4) the type of credit; and (5) institutional differences. Differences in the type of credit based on a purpose or collateral classification seem to contribute to differences in costs, but are difficult to disentangle from elements of size and risk.

Consumer finance companies reported the highest average operating cost per $100 of credit and showed the highest average cost in every listed category of expenditures (Table 29). At the other extreme, credit unions showed the lowest average cost on every item of expenditure except bad-debt losses and miscellaneous expenses. Commercial banks showed the lowest bad-debt losses and miscellaneous expenses.

METHOD OF ACQUIRING BUSINESS

Sales finance companies purchase most of their credit contracts from automobile dealers (indirect paper), while consumer finance companies and credit unions deal directly with the borrower (direct paper). Commercial banks obtain their receivables from both sources. The expenses incurred in the two methods of acquiring paper are very different.

Indirect financing frequently involves an arrangement whereby the dealer obtains a share of the finance charge. This share, which represents a part of the finance charge in automobile financing, amounted to an estimated 18 per cent of the gross charges at sales finance companies and 6 per cent at commercial banks.[2] The difference in importance of the dealer's share at these two types of institutions reflects differences in the proportion of their receivables in automobile credit and the share acquired indirectly.

The income received by dealers from finance charges may be used to cover their costs in initiating the contract or the risks that they assume. It also gives them some flexibility in their pricing and, under competitive market conditions, the dealer's share of the finance charge may be returned in part to credit buyers in the form of lower automobile prices. Thus gross finance charges shown in the first line of Table 29 may overstate the effective finance charge to this extent.

The dealer's finance income may be offset in part by a reduction in the financing agency's operating expenses. The dealer absorbs part of the risk on recourse contracts, which carry the highest dealer finance charge share. The dealer also absorbs some of the cost of originating and accepting the application. However, separate data on operating expenses of direct versus indirect operations suggest that the savings in handling costs on indirect paper are relatively small. Expense data from a subsample of banks covered by the study showed only minor differences between the costs of direct and indirect automobile paper. This evidence is supported by data collected by the American Bankers Association that show a differential of only 10 to 15 per cent between the acquisition costs of an automobile contract purchased from a dealer and one acquired directly.[3] These data show an average acquisition cost of $12.75 per contract on direct loans and $11.50 on indirect paper in 1957.

Direct lending agencies, such as consumer finance companies and banks, must attract business from the public. This involves more advertising and a different promotional approach from that used in acquiring paper from dealers. The sample consumer finance companies spent 89 cents per $100 of loans on advertising while commercial banks spent 34 cents per $100. The sales finance company figure, which was only slightly below that for commercial banks, includes some advertising for direct loans, as 20 per cent of their business was conducted directly with the public. The sales finance company with the largest advertising expense also had the largest direct loan operation.

---

[2] See note b, Table 29.

[3] Mimeographed material distributed by the Instalment Credit Commission of the American Bankers Association to their membership.

Direct lending agencies must also provide facilities that are convenient for the borrower. This not only requires additional offices but frequently more expensive locations. Consumer finance companies with loans of more than $100 million had an average of 500 offices per company in mid-1960, while sales finance companies in the same group averaged 200 offices per company.[4] Occupancy costs amounted to $1.09 per $100 of consumer credit at sample consumer finance companies and to only 43 cents per $100 at sales finance companies.

Although the sample banks obtained 75 per cent of their consumer credit business from the public, they reported lower average occupancy costs than sales finance companies. This difference may reflect the ability of the bank to spread the cost of occupancy among its many functions. Most finance companies must allocate nearly all the cost of quarters to their consumer credit business.

The extremely low occupancy cost at credit unions reflects the free space that is frequently provided by the sponsors of these organizations and the nominal space requirements associated with part time operations.

RISK

Some of the costs arising from risks are indicated by losses charged off and by provision for losses. These measures differ from year to year, with provisions for losses exceeding actual losses in all but very bad years, but they show the same pattern of costs over time. Neither of these measures includes losses sustained by dealers under recourse agreements, nor do they reflect differentials in costs of investigation and collection associated with variations in credit quality. They are, therefore, an incomplete measure of total costs of risks, and they understate the cost differential associated with different degrees of risk.

Loss figures, however, suggest the wide range of risks among lending institutions, as well as among individual companies. Actual losses charged off (net of recoveries) in 1959 varied from 15 cents per $100 of credit at commercial banks to more than ten times that amount, or $1.70 per $100 at consumer finance companies. Sales finance companies showed losses of $1.11 per $100, and credit unions of 38 cents per $100.

Many of the costs of handling higher-risk loans cannot be segregated from the rest of operating expenses. If all the costs associated with variations in risk could be isolated, risks would undoubtedly play a

---

[4] F. R. Pawley, "Survey of Finance Companies, Mid-1960," *Federal Reserve Bulletin,* October 1961, pp. 1154–1155.

substantial part in explaining differences in operating costs among lenders.

The volume of work required in handling and processing instalment contracts is more closely related to the number of contracts than to the dollar amounts involved. A subsample of banks, for example, handled thirty appliance contracts for every $10,000 in volume but only five automobile contracts for the same dollar volume.[5] The cost of handling $100 of appliance paper was accordingly much higher than the cost of handling the same dollar volume of automobile paper. Cost figures from these banks showed operating expenses of $7.40 per $100 for appliance paper and $3.09 per $100 for indirect automobile paper.

The average size of contracts acquired during the year varied among institutions from $436 at consumer finance companies to $1,031 at commercial banks (Table 30). These averages reflect the type of business conducted, as well as the size of contract by type of credit. The estimated average personal loan contract acquired by finance companies was only $431, compared with the average indirect automobile contract of $1,875 at commercial banks. The latter estimate includes both new- and used-car credit contracts.

Both the cost of acquiring new contracts during the year and the cost of servicing and handling old contracts are intermingled in the annual expense data obtained in this study. As a result, dividing annual expenses by the number of contracts acquired does not give a very good measure of the costs of acquiring an individual credit contract. Nor does dividing annual expenses by the number of outstanding contracts give a very good measure of the cost of handling and servicing credit contracts. However, such averages do give some indication of the influence of size of contract on costs. Estimates of the cost per outstanding contract, shown in the last column of Table 30, reveal that the percentage range of costs among different types of institutions is greatly reduced when costs are expressed per contract.

The high dollar cost per $100 of credit of consumer finance companies is clearly related to the small average size of contract. The differences between operating costs at consumer finance companies and other lenders are sharply reduced when the comparison is based on the cost per outstanding contract rather than on cost per $100 of credit. Consumer finance company costs per $100 of credit are three and a half times

[5] These figures are based on data from a subsample of five of the total bank sample.

TABLE 30

ANNUAL OPERATING EXPENSES BY TYPE OF INSTITUTION
AND SELECTED TYPES OF CREDIT, 1959
(dollars)

Type of Institution	Cost Per $100 of Credit Outstanding[a]	Average Size of Contract		Cost Per Contract Outstanding[d]
		Acquired[b]	Outstanding[c]	
		ALL TYPES OF CREDIT		
Nine consumer finance companies[e]	14.25	436	346	49.30
Ten sales finance companies[e]	7.74	896	700	54.18
Nine commercial banks[e]	4.17	1,031	723	30.15
All federal credit unions	3.30	593	553	18.25
		SELECTED TYPES OF CREDIT		
Nineteen finance companies:				
Automobile contracts	5.26[f]	1,768	1,149	60.44
Personal loans	14.42	431	341	49.17
Five commercial banks:				
Automobile paper, indirect	3.09	1,875	1,181	36.49
Automobile paper, direct	2.84	1,692	1,066	30.27
Modernization loans	3.49	1,403	909	31.72
Personal loans	4.36	714	468	20.40
Other goods paper	7.40	335	220	16.28

Source: Based on samples described in source to Table 29.

a
Data for group totals from Table 29, line 4.

b Obtained by dividing the dollar volume of contracts acquired by the number of contracts acquired during the year.

c
Obtained by dividing the amount outstanding (average of beginning and end of year) by the number of contracts outstanding (average of beginning and end of year).

d
Obtained by multiplying the cost per $100 of credit (col. 1) by the average outstanding contract (col. 3); equivalent to total operating expenses divided by average number of contracts outstanding at beginning and end of year.

e Average balances of contracts acquired and outstanding were obtained by weighting the average balances by type of credit by estimates of the number of contracts acquired and outstanding.

f Estimates of the cost of automobile contracts and of all other contracts were obtained by assuming that the cost per $100 for automobile contracts was the same at both consumer and sales finance companies and that the cost per $100 for all other contracts (largely personal loans) was also the same at each type of institution. That is, it was assumed that the over-all average costs per $100 differ only because of the difference in the proportions of auto and other contracts outstanding. If a is the cost per $100 of automobile contracts and b the cost per $100 of other contracts, and these are weighted by the relative proportions of amounts outstanding, then $.019a + .981b = \$14.25$ (for nine consumer finance companies), and $.729a + .271b = \$7.74$ (for ten sales finance companies). Hence $a = \$5.26$ and $b = \$14.42$.

those of banks and nearly twice those of sales finance companies but their costs per outstanding contract are only one and a half times those of commercial banks and are smaller than those of sales finance companies.

Data for commercial banks show a wide variation in cost by type of credit (Table 30). Operating expenses on direct automobile paper were $2.84 per $100, compared with $7.40 per $100 on other goods paper. These differences reflect many elements, such as risk, contract size, the number of instalments, and others that cannot be identified from available data. Such marked cost differentials within the same institutional structure suggest that some of the variation in costs among different types of institutions can be attributed to variations in the type of credit they extend.

The cost differential on the same type of business between types of institutions is sizable. The cost of providing personal loans at finance companies was nearly $10 per $100 more than at commercial banks, and nearly $11 per $100 more than at credit unions. Part, but not all, of these differentials can be explained by differences in average size of loan. The cost per contract was higher at finance companies than at other institutions, but the percentage spread was much smaller than the range in costs per dollar.

The expenses of all lenders are shaped to some extent by the legal and institutional framework within which they operate. The operating expenses of credit unions, for example, are reduced in a number of ways by their cooperative organization. Much of the clerical work is done by the voluntary help of the members, sometimes during time paid for by the sponsoring organization. Quarters are frequently provided by the sponsoring organization, and promotional expenses are usually nominal because of the limited membership. A quantitative comparison of the savings that result from these advantages is not possible. A rough indication of the nature of the differences is obtained by comparing the credit union costs with those of the sample of commercial banks. Commercial bank salary costs were a third larger, and their occupancy and advertising expenses were four times larger than those of credit unions.

The business conducted by consumer finance companies resembles that of credit unions in many ways. Both types of institutions deal primarily in relatively small personal loans, but their expenses differ widely. Salary expenses of consumer finance companies were three and a half times those of credit unions. Their occupancy costs were seventeen times larger, and their advertising expenses were twelve times larger.

The institutional advantages and disadvantages of other types of companies are less obvious and hence more difficult to detect. Regulations that specify operating procedures or legal restrictions that limit the size of loan may adversely affect expense ratios. The impact of regulatory provisions on consumer finance companies probably provides the best illustration of the cost differential arising from legal and administrative supervision. The adverse effect of their small loan size on expenses has already been discussed. Administrative provisions such as those requiring the issuance of new certificates and the cancellation of old ones upon the renewal of the loan and those specifying the daily computation of interest charges, add to the high cost of their operations.

INDIVIDUAL COMPANY VARIATIONS

As would be expected, individual companies of each type of institution differ considerably from an average for all companies. Many of the factors explaining differences in operating expense among different types of institutions apply to individual institutions. They operate in different markets and assume different credit risks, specialize in different types of credit, and work with varying degrees of efficiency.

A comparison of expense data for companies that show extremes in costs reveals considerable overlapping among types of institutions (Chart 10). The lowest-cost consumer finance company had lower operating expenses than did the highest-cost sales finance company. The lowest-cost sales finance company had lower costs than did the highest-cost commercial bank, and the bank with the lowest cost fell below the average for all federal credit unions.

Variations in Nonoperating Expenses

Nonoperating costs include the cost of nonequity funds, provisions for income taxes, and the lender's profit. Differences in costs among the four types of institutions reflect primarily different sources of funds and, in the case of federal credit unions, exemption from income taxes (Table 29). These costs contributed significantly to variations in gross

CHART 10
Individual Company Variations in Operating Expenses, 1959
(per $100 of average outstanding credit)

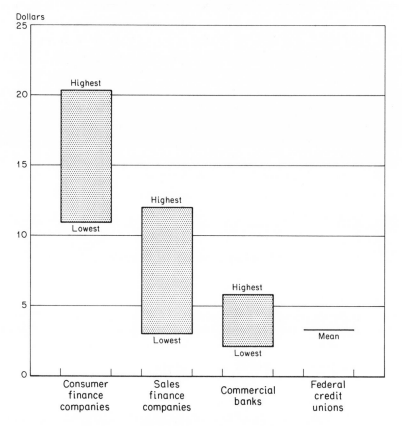

SOURCE: Bureau of Federal Credit Unions and sample data obtained for study.
NOTE: Includes dealer's share of gross finance charges.

finance charges among the four types of institutions, although they were less important than operating expenses in explaining these variations.

A number of factors contributed to differences in total nonoperating costs and to the distribution of these costs: (1) the rate paid for funds, in both the equity and nonequity markets; (2) sources and uses of funds, i.e., the proportion of funds supplied by owners and the proportion of resources held idle in nonearning assets; and (3) effective income tax rates.

RATE PAID FOR FUNDS

The institutions covered by this study draw their funds from the entire spectrum of credit markets and attract funds with a wide range of rates and terms. They do not all have access to the same markets, however, and their costs vary accordingly.

Commercial banks have exclusive access to demand deposits as a source of funds. They do not pay interest on these deposits but they assume a substantial part of the costs of handling and servicing these accounts. In addition, they bear hidden costs that cannot be measured, such as loss of earnings that result from holding legal reserves and from the low return on secondary reserves. The cost estimates of demand deposits are based on cost accounting records, and information was not available from the reporting banks to permit a separation of the costs of handling demand and time deposits.[6] The combined administrative cost of handling deposits at the sample banks, net of service charges, amounted to 70 cents per $100 of deposits (Table 31).

Both commercial banks and credit unions have access to the market for savings accounts. The cost of these accounts includes interest payment, as well as handling costs. The savings market covered by commercial banks and credit unions cannot be equated, however, because of the greater security offered by the commercial banks through deposit insurance and the debt status of their deposits. Savings accounts placed in credit unions must share many of the risks of equity capital. The sample commercial banks paid an average of 2.7 per cent on their time deposits in 1959 in contrast to cash payments of 3.4 per cent by federal credit unions.[7] In addition, the total cost of share accounts at credit unions includes the cost of servicing the accounts, retained earnings, and the costs of free insurance provided for shareholders. The total cost of the shareholders' funds in this broad view averaged 5 per cent.

All four types of financial institutions obtained some funds from various debt markets. Commercial banks borrow from other banks and from Federal Reserve banks. Since they typically pay off such borrow-

---

[6] An alternate method of estimating the cost of funds to commercial banks would require estimating the opportunity cost of credit to the consumer credit department of a bank. The cost accounting approach was chosen to avoid the arbitrary aspects of an opportunity-cost estimate.

[7] Insured commercial banks on the average paid a slightly lower figure (2.4 per cent) in 1959 (*Annual Report of the Federal Deposit Insurance Corporation for the Year Ended December 31, 1960*, Washington, 1961, pp. 154–155).

TABLE 31

AVERAGE COST OF FUNDS BY SOURCE AND TYPE OF INSTITUTION, 1959
(per cent of average outstanding balances)

Type of Institution	Debt and Deposits	Total Nonequity Funds	Equity Funds		
			Ratio of Net Profits (or Net Income)[a] to Equity Funds	Ratio of Dividends to Equity Funds	
Nine commercial banks, total	1.3[b]	1.2[b]	7.6	4.5	
Interest on time deposits	2.7	--	--	--	
Cost of handling deposits	.7	--	--	--	
Nine consumer finance companies	5.0	4.6	12.1	7.7	
Ten sales finance companies	4.5	4.2	10.3	5.9	
All federal credit unions	3.8	3.1	5.0	3.4	

Source: Based on samples described in source to Table 29.

[a] Because of differences in ownership and objectives, the term net profit is usually not used for credit unions. The term net income is used instead.

[b] Includes interest on debt.

ings before statement dates, the data for year-end dates seldom indicate the normal extent of this type of indebtedness. Rates on funds obtained in these markets correspond closely to Federal Reserve discount rates, which ranged between 3 and 4 per cent in 1959. Credit unions borrow relatively small amounts from banks and other credit unions. They paid an average of 3.8 per cent on their debt in 1959.

Finance companies obtain their funds from banks and from public markets. The large finance companies have access to nearly all of the public markets, both long- and short-term. Some of them place commercial paper directly with financial and nonfinancial corporations, others sell their paper through dealers. They raise long-term funds in the form of either subordinated or senior debt in the capital markets and by direct placement. In 1959 the sample of sales finance companies paid an average of 4.5 per cent for their debt funds obtained in all markets, while the consumer finance companies paid an average of 5 per cent.

Variations in the rate paid for total nonequity funds depend on the credit rating of the individual institution, the sources used, the mix between long- and short-term funds, and the importance of noninterest-bearing liabilities. The average rate paid by individual sales finance companies varied from 3.7 to 4.7 per cent and that paid by consumer finance companies varied from 4.0 to 5.6 per cent.

Since most banks require finance companies to maintain compensating balances, the average rate on finance company indebtedness understates the total costs. The added cost appears in this study as part of the costs of idle funds, since the compensating balances are included as bank balances.[8] This treatment is consistent with that used for bank reserves against deposits.

Equity funds used by banks and finance companies are obtained from local and national markets. The rate that must be earned on the book value of equity funds to attract new funds and the dividends that must be paid depends on the investor's attitude toward a particular company or type of business. The ratio of net profit to equity funds varied from 12.1 per cent for the sample of consumer finance companies to 7.6 per cent for banks (Table 31). Individual company variations in the return on equity were sizable.

---

[8] The cost of nonequity funds expressed as a percentage of consumer receivables (Table 29, line 12) reflects the cost of compensating balances, in that the total cost of funds is related to the proportion of funds that is actually invested in receivables.

SOURCES AND USES OF FUNDS

The proportion of total resources obtained from nonequity sources has an important impact on both the total cost of funds and upon the return to the lender. The percentage of nonequity funds used varied from 90 at commercial banks to 3 at credit unions (Table 32). The sample sales finance companies obtained 84 per cent and the consumer finance companies about 75 per cent of their funds from nonequity sources.

Since a share of the funds used in any lending operation must be allocated to cash balances and other nonearning assets, the cost of such funds reduces the return available from earning assets. Many accountants deduct the amount of nonearning assets from the total debt in computing the effective rate paid for funds used in their lending operations. Since the proportion of idle funds differed so widely from one type of institution to another, the costs of nonearning assets were treated in this study as a separate item of expense. In many cases, however, part of the expense of nonearning assets could be treated as a cost of non-

TABLE 32

SOURCES AND USES OF FUNDS BY TYPE OF INSTITUTION, 1959
(per cent)

Item	Nine Consumer Finance Companies	Ten Sales Finance Companies	Nine Commercial Banks	All Federal Credit Unions
Sources:				
Nonequity	74.6	84.2	90.2	2.6
Equity	25.4	15.8	9.8	97.4
Total	100.0	100.0	100.0	100.0
Uses:				
Earning assets, net	87.2	88.0	77.1	92.2
Nonearning assets	12.8	12.0	22.9	7.8
Total	100.0	100.0	100.0	100.0

Source: Based on averages of beginning- and end-of-year dates for samples described in source to Table 29.

equity funds. The large legal reserves required of banks could be considered in part as a cost of deposits, and the compensating balances that banks require of finance companies could be considered as part of the cost of borrowing.

The proportion of resources held in nonearning forms varied from 23 per cent for the sample of banks to 8 per cent at federal credit unions. Finance companies of both types held about 12 to 13 per cent of their resources in nonearning forms (Table 32).

COST OF NONEQUITY FUNDS

The cost of nonequity funds used in consumer credit varied between $4.02 per $100 of credit at sales finance companies to 12 cents per $100 at federal credit unions (Table 29). These differences reflected variations in the rates paid for these funds, in the proportion of nonequity funds used for consumer credit, and in the burden of nonearning assets.

The average cost of nonequity funds to lenders fell within a relatively narrow range except for commercial banks (Table 31). Finance companies and credit unions paid between 3.1 and 4.6 per cent, whereas the banks paid an average of 1.2 per cent.

The cost of nonequity funds used in consumer credit includes the burden of providing part of the funds used in nonearning forms. Many companies deduct their nonearning assets from nonequity funds in computing the effective rate paid for funds used in lending operations. When nonearning assets take a relatively large share of total resources, the effective cost of money will be considerably higher than the rate paid for the funds. The cost of nonearning assets is relatively most important at commercial banks, where idle funds add about 40 per cent to the effective cost of money used in lending (Table 33).

Since the average cost of nonequity funds used in consumer lending also depends on the extent to which these funds are used, the proportion of nonequity to equity funds affects the total cost of such funds as a percentage of consumer receivables. The extremely low cost of nonequity funds at credit unions merely reflects the minor importance of such funds in their total resources, while the high cost at finance companies reflects the importance of nonequity funds.

The various elements entering into the cost of nonequity funds as a part of the gross finance charge are summarized in Table 33. Although the average rate paid for nonequity funds by consumer finance companies was higher than that paid by sales finance companies, the net cost to the consumer was about the same because of the difference in the share

TABLE 33

COST OF NONEQUITY FUNDS BY TYPE OF INSTITUTION, 1959
(per cent of average outstanding balances)

Ratio of Dollar Cost of Nonequity Funds to:	Nine Consumer Finance Companies	Ten Sales Finance Companies	Nine Commercial Banks	All Federal Credit Unions
Total debt and deposits	5.0	4.5	1.3	3.8
Total nonequity funds	4.6	4.2	1.2	3.1
Nonequity funds minus nonearning assets	5.6	4.8	1.7	a
Consumer credit receivables[b]	4.0	4.0	1.5	.1

Source: Based on samples described in source to Table 29.
a
Nonearning assets exceed nonequity funds at federal credit unions.
b
Table 29, cost of nonequity funds.

of equity funds used. The low cost of nonequity funds to consumers at commercial banks, despite the importance of these funds in their total resources, reflects the lower cost of these funds to the bank.

INCOME TAXES

The most striking variation in income tax arises from the tax exemption of credit unions as cooperative organizations. The other three types of institutions are all subject to income taxes.

Among the three taxpaying institutions, the sample of consumer finance companies reported the highest tax cost—$2.73 per $100— and sales finance companies the lowest—$1.07 per $100. The differences reflected primarily their earnings before tax. The effective rate on pre-tax earnings averaged 45 per cent at all three types. The percentage varied slightly by type of institution but the differences were small and might have been caused by adjustments for over- or underaccruals in previous years or other special tax adjustments rather than by different effective rates.

COST OF EQUITY FUNDS

The cost of equity funds (lender's profit) from consumer credit ranged from 81 cents per $100 of consumer credit at sales finance companies to about seven times that amount, or $5.71 per $100, at federal credit unions (Table 29). These differences reflect variations in the ability of lenders to convert the return from their lending into a satisfactory return on equity and the return from consumer credit that has to be maintained to provide an adequate return on net worth to attract and hold funds in the business. The total cost of equity funds to the consumer falls well below the return on equity funds. For example, consumers paid 81 cents per $100 for the use of equity funds at sales finance companies in 1959, yet the return on equity funds (net profits to equity funds) at these companies was $10 per $100. Sales finance companies earned a net operating income from consumer credit of 5.9 per cent and, after interest but before taxes, were able to earn 18 per cent on their net worth.

The principal device for enlarging the return from consumer lending lies in the financial advantage or leverage of the use of nonequity funds. If the lender can earn a higher return on his resources than he pays for the funds, the differential profit accrues to the owners and enlarges the return. This advantage permits the lender to charge the consumer less for the use of equity than he has to earn to attract risk capital into the business.

All stockholder-owned institutions depended heavily on the financial advantage of nonequity funds to produce a satisfactory return on equity from the relatively low equity cost to the consumer (Table 34). Leverage was highest at commercial banks where 83 per cent of the return on equity came from the use of nonequity funds, the next highest at sales finance companies, and the lowest at consumer finance companies where 59 per cent of the return was from this source. The high cost of equity funds to the credit union borrowers can be explained almost entirely by the absence of financial advantage from the use of debt.

All four types of institutions invested part of their resources in nonconsumer activities. Commercial banks and credit unions showed a lower return from all earning assets than from consumer assets alone (Table 34, lines 1 and 2). At the sample commercial banks, the average net operating income on all earning assets was 3.4 per cent, or 1.9 percentage points less than the yield on consumer assets. At the credit unions, the net operating income on all earning assets was .5 of a percentage point below the return on consumer credit. Consumer credit activities therefore carry more than a proportionate share in the total cost of equity funds at these institutions.

The sample sales finance companies, however, earned a higher aver-

TABLE 34

FACTORS IN LENDER'S PROFITS BY TYPE OF INSTITUTION, 1959
(per cent of average outstanding balances)

Ratio	Nine Consumer Finance Companies	Ten Sales Finance Companies	Nine Commercial Banks	All Federal Credit Unions
1. Net operating income from consumer credit to consumer receivables	9.6	5.9	5.3	5.8
2. Net operating income to earning assets	10.4	7.2	3.4	5.3
3. Net operating income to total assets	9.1	6.3	2.5	4.9
4. Profits before taxes to equity funds[a]	22.2	17.9	14.5	5.0
5. Net return from nonequity to equity funds (line 4 minus line 3)	13.1	11.6	12.0	0.1
6. Provision for income taxes to profit before taxes	45.8	42.5	46.0	--
7. Net profits to equity funds[a]	12.1	10.3	7.6	5.0
8. Percentage of profit obtained from leverage on nonequity funds (line 5 ÷ line 4)	59.0	64.8	82.7	0.9[b]
ALTERNATIVE DERIVATION OF LINE 5				
a. Net operating income to total assets (line 3)	9.1	6.3	2.5	4.9
less				
b. Cost of nonequity funds to nonequity funds	4.6	4.2	1.2	3.1
equals				
c. Net return from nonequity funds to nonequity funds	4.5	2.1	1.3	1.8
times				
d. Leverage coefficient (ratio of nonequity to equity funds)	3.0	5.6	9.6	0.03
equals				
e. Net return from nonequity to equity funds (line 5)[c]	13.5	11.8	12.5	0.05

Source: Based on samples described in source to Table 29. Items 1 and 7 are based on data in Tables 29 and 31, respectively.

[a] Based on net income to equity for federal credit unions.

[b] Based on unrounded data.

[c] Differences between lines 5 and e result from rounding errors introduced by alternative methods of calculation.

age return (1.3 percentage points higher) on their total earning assets than on their consumer assets. Part of this difference may reflect the difficulty of adjusting the sales finance cost data to allow properly for the cost of nonconsumer credit. Provision was made for the cost of insurance and other nonconsumer operations, but such costs are difficult to segregate, and some of the related costs may have been underestimated.

Profitable alternatives for the use of funds permit some flexibility in the pricing of consumer credit for some companies. To the extent that the higher earnings rate on other earning assets arises from activities related to consumer lending, such as credit life insurance or insurance on the collateral to the loan, the lender can offer lower rates on credit. In such cases, part of the cost of consumer credit may be absorbed in other activities and paid for in the form of higher prices for the related items. This type of substitution is common in retail operations, where part of the cost of credit may be absorbed in the price of the article sold. The possibility of substitution makes an exact determination of the total cost of credit to consumers virtually impossible.

COMPARISON BY TYPE OF INSTITUTION

Nonoperating expenses on consumer credit were highest at the sample of consumer finance companies. Their high cost compared to other types of institutions reflected their tax disadvantage relative to credit unions; the high cost of their nonequity funds; their small ratio of non-equity funds to total resources, which, together with their high cost of funds, resulted in the lowest leverage among the stockholder-owned institutions; and the high cost of their equity funds.

At the other extreme, the commercial bank sample had the lowest nonoperating costs. They were $4.37 per $100 below those of the consumer finance companies and reflected primarily the low cost of their nonequity funds and their high ratio of nonequity funds to total resources, which, together with their low cost of funds, gave them the largest advantage from leverage.

Federal credit unions had the second lowest nonoperating costs. Their position relative to finance companies stemmed primarily from their exemption from income taxes and their inexpensive source of equity funds from the savings markets.

The sample of sales finance companies showed nonoperating costs of $2.70 per $100 less than those of the consumer finance companies, despite the many similarities in their operations. They were able to achieve this cost differential largely because: (1) they were able to supplement their earnings from consumer credit by a high rate of return on their other activities; (2) they obtained a slightly better rate on non-equity funds; (3) they had a high ratio of nonequity funds to total resources and hence were able to show greater leverage; and (4) their cost of equity funds was smaller.

Rate of Profits[9]

The lenders' profits are a necessary cost to consumers as long as they are no larger than needed to attract and hold equity funds in the industry. The profits from consumer credit would be considered "normal" if they were similar to those of their competitors for equity funds. Such comparisons are difficult because of a wide variety of factors that enter into the market evaluation of equities. The rate that any company or any type of institution must earn depends on the investor's appraisal of the risks involved, potential growth, and his attitude toward the industry and the particular company.

The extremes in the market for equity funds are illustrated by the difference between the sources of funds for credit unions and those for consumer finance companies. Credit unions offer a high degree of liquidity with some risk, while the stock of a finance company may offer less liquidity and greater risk. Investors in the latter case must be compensated by a higher return.

The average net profit to the book value of equity funds in 1959, shown in Table 34, ranged from 5 per cent at federal credit unions to 7.6 per cent at the sample commercial banks, 10.3 per cent at the sales finance companies, and 12.1 per cent at the consumer finance companies. Although these averages vary with the gross finance charges at these institutions, this does not imply excessive profits in any case. The normal return would be expected to vary with liquidity, risk, the growth potential, and the investor appeal of the different types of institutions.

All the profit rates for the stockholder-owned financial institutions fell well within the range of rates at manufacturing corporations.[10] The average profit to equity funds for the samples of stockholder-owned companies covered by the study was 9.9 per cent in 1959, compared with an average for all manufacturing corporations of 10.4 per cent.

[9] The term "net income" has been used to indicate the return after expenses for federal credit unions instead of net profits because of differences in the ownership and objectives of credit unions.

[10] *Quarterly Financial Report for Manufacturing Corporations, First Quarter 1960,* Federal Trade Commission and Securities and Exchange Commission, pp. 12–27.

The profit rates for a number of industry groups, including the chemical, drug, and tobacco industries, were higher than the highest rate for institutions covered by the study. These comparisons cannot necessarily establish the profits of consumer lending as normal, but they place consumer credit institutions in an intermediate position among their competitors for equity capital.

CHAPTER 7

Trends in Cost of Providing Consumer Credit

THE years covered by this study encompassed two periods of federal controls on instalment credit terms and three minor recessions. The period opened in the recession year of 1949 and closed in 1959, the first year of recovery after the 1958 recession. The period as a whole, however, was one of rapid growth in consumer credit. The recessions were merely interludes in a strong upward trend in outstanding credit.

The outstanding amount of consumer credit tripled during the 1950's and all segments of the industry participated in the expansion. The share of total instalment credit held by financial institutions increased somewhat at the expense of holdings by retailers. An increase in the share held by credit unions absorbed most of the gain in the total held by financial institutions. The proportion of the total held by other types of financial institutions showed little change.

The diversity of economic events and the brevity of the time span dictate caution in interpreting trends that appear in the cost data. Two general observations may be made about developments during this period. First, average charges for consumer credit were generally lower at the end of the 1950's than at the beginning. Second, the spread in average finance charges between high- and low-cost institutions was reduced during this period.

Average finance charges declined appreciably between 1949 and 1955 at sales and consumer finance companies, and rose modestly at federal credit unions (Table 35). Commercial bank data were not available for this period. Between 1955 and 1959, average finance charges of consumer finance companies and credit unions declined slightly, and those of commercial banks and sales finance companies rose. For the period as a whole, average charges of both groups of finance companies declined and the credit union charge showed a slight drop. By 1959 charges at consumer finance companies and credit unions were the lowest of any year in the period covered. The decline in sales finance company charges resulted from a decline in average charges on both automobile credit and personal loans. To a considerable extent the decline in automobile credit reflects a narrowing of the spread of charges between high- and low-cost companies in the sample, the rates of the two lowest-cost companies rising slightly and those of the high-cost companies declining appreciably. As the low-cost companies held a greater portion of receivables than the high-cost companies, a weighted average of rates of charge per dollar of receivables shows a substantially lower level and a

TABLE 55

AVERAGE FINANCE CHARGES ON CONSUMER CREDIT, 1949, 1955, AND 1959
(dollars per $100 of average outstanding credit)

TYPE OF CREDIT AND INSTITUTION	Simple Averages[a]			Weighted Averages[b]			CHANGE			
							1949 to 1959		1955 to 1959	
	1949	1955	1959	1949	1955	1959	Simple Average	Weighted Average	Simple Average	Weighted Average
All types:										
Consumer finance companies[c]	26.10	24.20	24.00	25.00	23.50	22.40	-2.10	-2.60	-.20	-1.10
Sales finance companies[c]	20.00	16.50	16.60	14.00	13.00	13.50	-3.40	-.50	+.10	+.50
Commercial banks[c]	n.a.	8.60	10.00	n.a.	9.50	10.10	n.a.	n.a.	+1.40	+.60
Federal credit unions	n.a.	n.a.	n.a.	9.40	9.60	9.10	n.a.	-.30	n.a.	-.50
Automobile credit:										
Sales finance companies[c]	20.40	15.00	15.80	14.30	12.90	13.70	-4.60	-.60	+.80	+.80
Commercial banks, indirect[c]	n.a.	10.30	10.60	n.a.	10.10	10.00	n.a.	n.a.	+.30	-.10
Commercial banks, direct	n.a.	10.40	8.80	n.a.	9.20	8.60	n.a.	n.a.	-1.60	-.60
Other goods paper, commercial banks	n.a.	10.00	11.20	n.a.	11.00	11.40	n.a.	n.a.	+1.20	+.40
Modernization loans, commercial banks	n.a.	6.60	9.00	n.a.	6.50	10.60	n.a.	n.a.	+2.40	+4.10
Personal loans:										
Consumer finance companies	27.50	25.60	24.90	25.70	23.80	22.50	-2.60	-3.20	-.70	-1.30
Sales finance companies	25.00	24.10	21.50	24.70	24.40	22.40	-3.50	-2.30	-2.60	-2.00
Commercial banks	n.a.	9.50	10.90	n.a.	10.90	10.60	n.a.	n.a.	+1.40	-.30
Federal credit unions	n.a.	n.a.	n.a.	9.40	9.60	9.10	n.a.	-.30	n.a.	-.50

a Average of charges for each company with each company treated as a unit.

b Charges of each company were weighted by its receivables in computing average.

c Includes dealer's share of the gross finance charges.

99

smaller decline than the simple average of rates of charge from sample companies.

The trend in finance charges at commercial banks, for which data are available only from 1955, was upward. The changes in the over-all average at commercial banks reflected a variety of trends in rates and changes in the type of loan activity. Finance charges on indirect automobile paper, other consumer goods paper, and modernization loans rose from 1955 to 1959 (Table 35). The increase was largest in modernization loans where charges rose several dollars per $100 from 1955 to 1959. Rates on other consumer goods paper also rose, but the proportion of this paper held by commercial banks was sharply reduced during the period. Personal loans increased in importance while the charges on these loans reflected mixed trends at the sample banks.

A number of developments during the 1950's contributed to the reduction in charges on consumer credit by sales and consumer finance companies. An increase in the average contract size affected finance charges in two ways: (1) the larger contract size reduced the per-dollar operating costs and permitted lower charges; and (2) under the graduated rate structure applied to consumer finance companies, the increase in loan size resulted in a decrease in the average maximum legal charge. Competition from lower-cost institutions also intensified as the number of banks and credit unions engaged in consumer lending expanded.

The spread between finance charges at the institutions with the highest and lowest charges was smaller—by $1 or $2 per $100 of outstanding credit—in 1959 than in 1949. Although charges at both the high- and low-cost institutions declined, the decrease was larger at the high-cost institutions—consumer finance companies (Table 35).

Operating Expenses

Operating expenses on consumer credit showed the same general pattern of change during the period as average finance charges shown in Chart 11, with somewhat larger year-to-year variations. The operating expenses of the two samples of finance companies declined directly with the decline in the average finance charge. Operating expenses at credit unions showed relatively little change, while those at commercial banks increased slightly from 1955 to 1959.

The operating expenses of consumer finance companies varied between 57 and 61 per cent of the finance charge, with the peak years occurring in the recession years of 1949 and 1958 (Chart 12). The fluctuations in operating expenses at sales finance companies were somewhat wider,

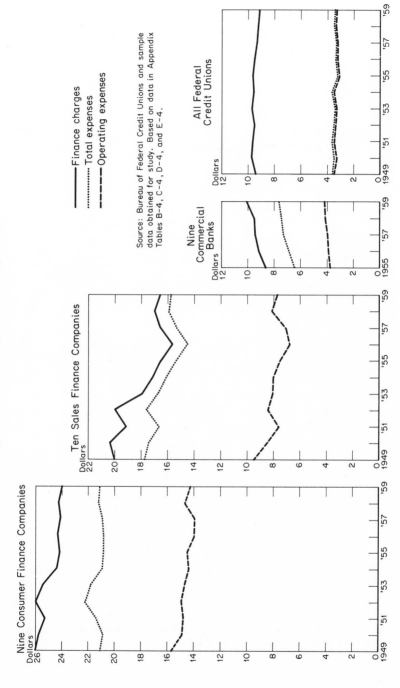

Average Finance Charges, Total Expenses, and Operating Expenses on Consumer Credit, by Type of Institution, 1949–59 (per $100 of average outstanding credit)

Finance charges
Total expenses
Operating expenses

Source: Bureau of Federal Credit Unions and sample data obtained for study. Based on data in Appendix Tables B-4, C-4, D-4, and E-4.

CHART 12

Operating Expenses on Consumer Credit as Percentage of
Finance Charges, by Type of Institution, 1949–59

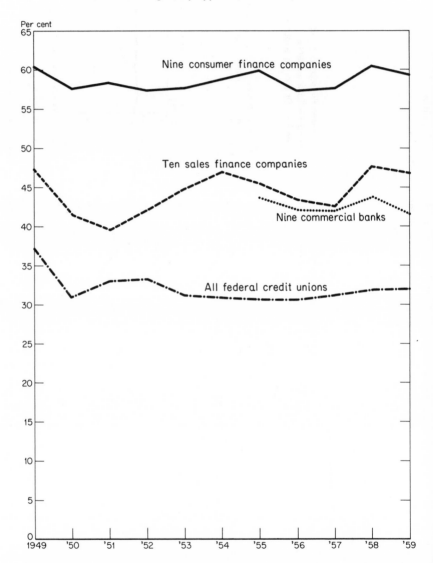

SOURCE: Bureau of Federal Credit Unions and sample data obtained for study. Based on data
in Appendix Tables B-4, C-4, D-4, and E-4.

varying between 40 and 48 per cent of total charges. The highest ratios occurred in the recession years of 1949, 1954, and 1958.

The decline in operating costs at finance companies resulted primarily from a decline in wage and salary payments. This decline was particularly striking in view of the general upward trend of wage rates during the period. Although data are not available on wage rates at finance companies, the average wage rate in retail trade rose by 50 per cent from 1949 to 1959 while salary payments per $100 of credit outstanding at sales finance companies declined by 15 per cent and those at consumer finance companies by 10 per cent (Chart 13). The reduction in salary costs indicates substantial savings on labor during this period.

Salary payments at commercial banks, however, rose slightly from 1955 to 1959 with the peak cost in 1958. The increase in salaries was not as large as the growth in wage rates during this period, so that some of the improved efficiency reflected in finance company operations was apparently enjoyed by banks.

The trend in advertising and promotional costs per $100 of credit outstanding varied widely among different types of institutions. The sample consumer finance companies reported a decline of 36 per cent during the period covered by the study, while sales finance companies reported an increase of about the same relative size (Table 36). The increase at sales finance companies probably reflects in part the extension of their direct lending. Consumer finance companies were still spending nearly three times as much on advertising as sales finance companies in 1959. The sample commercial banks reported a sizable increase in advertising expenditures in 1955–59 and during this period passed sales finance companies in expenditures on advertising per $100 of credit.

Actual losses on bad debts and provision for losses varied so widely from year to year that no clear trends for the over-all period were apparent. Actual losses (net of recoveries) were highest in 1949, 1953, and 1958. Provision for losses, as would be expected, were much more stable than actual losses, but conformed in general to the pattern of actual losses.

Nonoperating Expenses

Sizable year-to-year fluctuations in nonoperating expenses made it difficult to confirm any trends in the data. Some downward trend appeared to exist in the nonoperating expenses of finance companies, as the averages of these expenses for the last few years of the study were

TABLE 36

OPERATING EXPENSES ON CONSUMER CREDIT, BY TYPE OF EXPENSE AND INSTITUTION, 1949–59

(dollars per $100 of average outstanding credit)

Item	1949	1950	1951	1952	1953	1954	1955	1956	1957	1958	1959
Total operating expenses:											
Nine consumer finance companies	15.72	14.87	14.77	14.94	14.66	14.36	14.46	13.94	13.93	14.64	14.25
Ten sales finance companies	9.45	8.46	7.56	8.37	8.04	8.03	7.52	6.78	7.03	8.06	7.74
Nine commercial banks	—	—	—	—	—	—	3.76	3.86	3.96	4.14	4.17
All federal credit unions	3.48	3.28	3.49	3.39	3.26	3.52	3.07	3.23	3.21	3.34	3.30
Salaries:											
Nine consumer finance companies	7.12	6.70	6.79	6.91	6.82	6.57	6.65	6.47	6.40	6.69	6.45
Ten sales finance companies	4.16	3.93	3.68	3.86	3.57	3.70	3.36	3.12	3.30	3.54	3.47
Nine commercial banks	—	—	—	—	—	—	2.11	2.23	2.33	2.38	2.33
All federal credit unions	2.10	1.93	2.05	2.06	1.90	1.85	1.82	1.80	1.80	1.79	1.77
Occupancy costs:											
Nine consumer finance companies	1.21	1.08	1.07	1.08	1.08	1.05	1.07	1.05	1.03	1.10	1.09
Ten sales finance companies	.43	.47	.41	.37	.40	.42	.40	.38	.39	.45	.43
Nine commercial banks[a]	—	—	—	—	—	—	.22	.21	.22	.23	.23
All federal credit unions[a]	—	—	—	—	—	—	—	.06	.06	.06	.06
Advertising:											
Nine consumer finance companies	1.38	1.25	1.24	1.14	1.03	.87	.97	.93	.85	.80	.89
Ten sales finance companies	.22	.25	.27	.26	.26	.28	.27	.28	.28	.30	.31
Nine commercial banks[a]	—	—	—	—	—	—	.24	.24	.23	.30	.34
All federal credit unions[a]	—	—	—	—	—	—	—	.08	.07	.07	.07
Provision for losses:											
Nine consumer finance companies	2.03	2.13	1.88	1.86	1.81	1.79	1.84	1.70	1.72	2.02	1.98
Ten sales finance companies	2.01	1.36	1.04	1.57	1.59	1.44	1.39	1.11	1.12	1.68	1.46
Nine commercial banks	—	—	—	—	—	—	.31	.28	.31	.28	.28

(continued)

TABLE 36 (concluded)

Item	1949	1950	1951	1952	1953	1954	1955	1956	1957	1958	1959
Actual losses (net of recoveries):											
Nine consumer finance companies	1.47	1.42	1.51	1.38	1.43	1.50	1.39	1.15	1.39	1.71	1.70
Ten sales finance companies	1.16	.73	.88	1.17	1.41	1.23	.83	.97	.95	1.77	1.11
Nine commercial banks	–	–	–	–	–	–	.13	.28	.33	.17	.15
All federal credit unions	.30	.27	.32	.23	.25	.56	.12	.31	.30	.41	.38
Miscellaneous expenses:											
Nine consumer finance companies	3.98	3.71	3.79	3.95	3.92	4.08	3.93	3.79	3.93	4.03	3.84
Ten sales finance companies	2.63	2.45	2.16	2.31	2.22	2.19	2.10	1.89	1.94	2.09	2.07
Nine commercial banks	–	–	–	–	–	–	.88	.90	.87	.95	.99
All federal credit unions [a]	1.08	1.08	1.12	1.10	1.11	1.11	1.13	.98	.98	1.01	1.02

[a]
Separate figures for occupancy and advertising costs were not available for federal credit unions prior to 1955. Before that date costs of these items are included in miscellaneous expenses.

CHART 13

Salary Expenses Per $100 of Average Outstanding Consumer Credit and Hourly Wage Rate, 1950–59

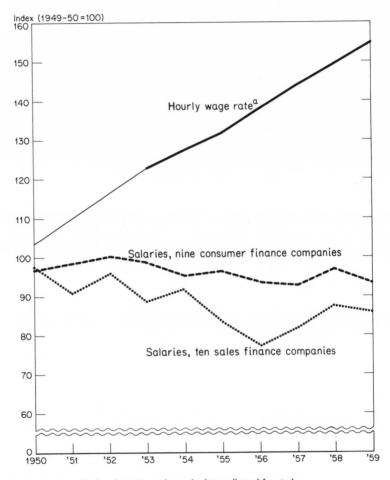

SOURCE: Bureau of Labor Statistics and sample data collected for study.
a For retail establishments.

below those of the earlier years. In contrast, the nonoperating expenses of commercial banks increased in most years between 1955 and 1959.

The distribution of these costs, however, changed markedly during the 1950's. The proportion of nonoperating costs going into nonequity funds increased sharply, while the share going to income taxes and to equity funds decreased accordingly. This trend was most pronounced at the two finance company groups but was visible to a lesser extent in the data for commercial banks (Chart 14). The cost of nonequity funds at consumer finance companies increased from 22 per cent of total non-operating expenses in 1949 to 41 per cent in 1959. The increase at sales finance companies was almost as large, from 40 to nearly 70 per cent. The cost of nonequity funds also increased slightly in importance at commercial banks during the last five years of the 1950's.

Although this shift in the components of cost had relatively little effect on the total cost of credit to consumers, it had important implications for the lending institutions. The decline in costs of equity funds as a percentage of the total finance charge resulted in a decline in the lenders' earnings on consumer credit receivables.

COST OF NONEQUITY FUNDS

The sharp rise in interest rates in the 1950's was the principal factor in the increase in the cost of nonequity funds. The prime commercial paper rate rose from less than 1 per cent in 1949 to an average of 4 per cent in 1959. The prime bank rate rose from 2.5 to 4.5 per cent and longer-term market rates rose as well.

The impact of the increase in interest rates fell most directly on finance companies because of their dependence on debt financing. That they did not pass all of the increased costs of funds on to the consumers is suggested by a decline in the cost of funds' share of the average finance charge paid by consumers. As a result, the higher costs of non-equity funds was reflected by a reduction in profits and was absorbed in a reduction in the cost of equity funds and tax payments.

The average cost of nonequity funds rose by 73 per cent from 1949 to 1959 at consumer finance companies and by 56 per cent at sales finance companies. This rise reflected both higher interest rates and the increase in the proportion of nonequity funds used.

The impact of higher interest rates was much less pronounced on commercial banks. Their costs were affected only insofar as they increased rates paid on time deposits. The average rate paid on time deposits by the sample commercial banks rose from less than 1.2 per cent in 1955 to 2.7 per cent in 1959, but their average cost of nonequity funds only increased from .9 to 1.2 per cent during the last five years of the 1950's.

Credit unions escaped the pressure of higher rates largely because nonequity funds played such a small role in their total operations. The rates that they paid for nonequity funds increased from 2.2 to 3.1 per

CHART 14
Nonoperating Expenses on Consumer Credit, by Type of Expense, 1949–59
(per $100 of average outstanding credit)

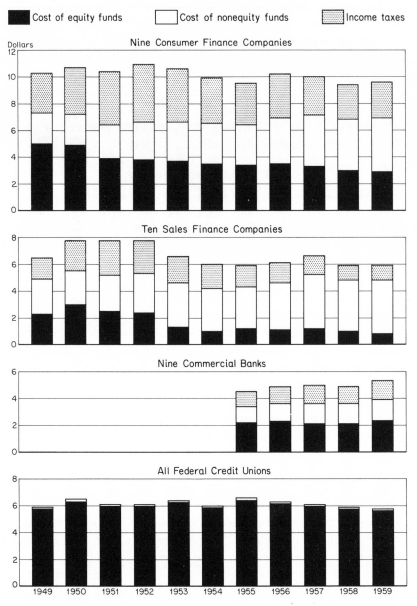

■ Cost of equity funds   ☐ Cost of nonequity funds   ▦ Income taxes

Nine Consumer Finance Companies

Ten Sales Finance Companies

Nine Commercial Banks

All Federal Credit Unions

1949 1950 1951 1952 1953 1954 1955 1956 1957 1958 1959

SOURCE: Bureau of Federal Credit Unions and sample data collected for study. Based on data in Appendix Tables B-4, C-4, D-4, and E-4.

108

cent. The over-all effect of higher interest rates on the cost of their lending operations was small.

Chart 11 shows the cost of equity funds as the difference between the gross finance charge and total expenses; it illustrates the changes during the period and the institutional differences in the importance of the cost of equity funds as a component of the gross finance charge. The decline in cost of equity funds (lender's profit) at finance companies was one of the most pronounced changes in the components of cost during the period. The cost of equity funds dropped from $4.97 per $100 of outstanding credit in 1949 to $2.92 in 1959 at consumer finance companies and from $2.31 to $.81 at sales finance companies. These declines stemmed largely from the increased use and cost of nonequity funds.

The sample banks and federal credit unions showed quite different trends in the cost of equity funds. These costs rose slightly at banks from 1955 to 1959 and were relatively stable throughout the eleven-year period at credit unions. The cost of equity funds at credit unions averaged $6 per $100 of credit outstanding with a year-to-year variation of plus or minus 6 or 7 per cent.

Lender's Rate of Profit

The cost of equity funds used in consumer lending is affected by the profit rate that is required to keep the lender in the business of providing credit to consumers and by the effectiveness with which the lender can convert the return from consumer credit into a satisfactory return on equity funds. The decline in the cost of equity funds to consumers at finance companies implied a reduction in their profits or compensating changes in earnings or costs. The over-all profitability, as noted earlier, depends on other uses of funds as well.

All of the companies in the samples had income from nonconsumer activities. The contribution of these activities to profits depends upon the return on the funds thus employed and on the proportion of funds used in these activities. Since it was beyond the scope of the study to analyze nonearning assets in detail, the impact of these activities on profits can only be indicated by a comparison of the average return on all earning assets and the average return on consumer receivables (Table 37).

TABLE 37

COMPARISON OF RETURN ON CONSUMER ASSETS AND ALL EARNING ASSETS BY TYPE OF INSTITUTION, 1949–59
(per cent of average outstanding balances)

Item	1949	1950	1951	1952	1953	1954	1955	1956	1957	1958	1959
1. Net operating income on all earning assets:											
Nine consumer finance companies	10.8	11.2	10.9	11.5	11.2	10.5	10.4	11.0	10.9	10.2	10.4
Ten sales finance companies	7.8	9.0	8.5	8.5	8.2	8.1	7.5	7.3	7.6	7.0	7.2
Nine commercial banks	–	–	–	–	–	–	2.5	2.9	3.3	3.4	3.4
All federal credit unions	4.8	5.4	5.0	5.2	5.5	5.3	5.7	5.5	5.5	5.3	5.3
2. Net operating income on consumer assets:											
Nine consumer finance companies	10.3	10.7	10.4	10.9	10.6	9.9	9.5	10.2	10.0	9.4	9.6
Ten sales finance companies	6.5	7.8	7.8	7.8	6.6	6.0	5.9	6.1	6.6	5.9	5.9
Nine commercial banks	–	–	–	–	–	–	4.5	4.9	5.0	4.9	5.3
All federal credit unions	5.9	6.5	6.1	6.1	6.4	6.0	6.6	6.3	6.1	5.9	5.8
3. Difference between items 1 and 2:											
Nine consumer finance companies	.5	.5	.5	.6	.6	.6	.9	.8	.9	.8	.8
Ten sales finance companies	1.3	1.2	.7	.7	1.6	2.1	1.6	1.2	1.0	1.1	1.3
Nine commercial banks	–	–	–	–	–	–	-2.0	-2.0	-1.7	-1.5	-1.9
All federal credit unions	-1.1	-1.1	-1.1	-.9	-.9	-.7	-.9	-.8	-.6	-.6	-.5

Finance companies of both types showed a higher return on total earning assets than on consumer assets. At consumer finance companies during the period studied, the spread between net operating income on all earning assets and on consumer assets increased from .5 to .8 of a percentage point from 1949 to 1959. This improvement in return from other activities reduced the effects of the loss of earnings per $100 of outstanding balances from their consumer activities. Sales finance companies showed a higher spread between their total earnings and consumer earnings than consumer finance companies, but there was no noticeable trend in the sales finance differential over the period.

Both commercial banks and credit unions showed a considerably smaller return on all earning assets than on consumer credit. The difference reflects in large part the liquidity and solvency requirements imposed by the nature of their liabilities and the legal restrictions on the investments of these institutions.

The rise in market interest rates permitted both commercial banks and credit unions to improve their earnings on total assets relative to consumer credit during the 1950's. Both types of institutions showed some reduction in the spread between net operating income on consumer assets and on all earning assets during this period (Table 37).

COST OF NONEARNING ASSETS

Finance companies and credit unions were able to reduce the proportion of nonearning assets to total assets during the 1950's, and thus to reduce the burden of these funds to their other operations (Table 38). Commercial banks, however, did not show any reduction in the relative size of their nonearning assets for 1955–59.

The imputed cost of these funds can be indicated by the difference between net operating income on earning assets and net operating income on total assets. The cost of these funds measured in this way declined at all types of lenders except commercial banks during the 1950's. Finance companies were able to reduce this cost by about 25 to 30 per cent by reducing the proportion of resources held in nonearning assets. This reduction was in part possible because of their reduced dependence on commercial bank borrowing with its compensatory balance requirements. The more effective use of their funds added to overall profits on total resources.

FINANCIAL ADVANTAGE OF USE OF NONEQUITY FUNDS

The net return to equity from the use of nonequity funds declined at both groups of finance companies during the fifties. This resulted from

TABLE 38

COST OF NONEARNING ASSETS BY TYPE OF INSTITUTION, 1949–59
(per cent of average outstanding balances)

Item	1949	1950	1951	1952	1953	1954	1955	1956	1957	1958	1959
1. Net operating income on all earning assets:											
Nine consumer finance companies	10.8	11.2	10.9	11.5	11.2	10.5	10.4	11.0	10.9	10.2	10.4
Ten sales finance companies	7.8	9.0	8.5	8.5	8.2	8.1	7.5	7.3	7.6	7.0	7.2
Nine commercial banks	—	—	—	—	—	—	2.5	2.9	3.3	3.4	3.4
All federal credit unions	4.8	5.4	5.0	5.2	5.5	5.3	5.7	5.5	5.5	5.3	5.3
2. Net operating income on total assets:											
Nine consumer finance companies	9.1	9.5	9.3	9.8	9.6	8.9	8.9	9.5	9.3	8.9	9.1
Ten sales finance companies	6.4	7.6	7.2	7.3	7.1	7.0	6.6	6.4	6.6	6.1	6.3
Nine commercial banks	—	—	—	—	—	—	1.9	2.1	2.4	2.5	2.5
All federal credit unions	4.3	4.8	4.5	4.6	4.9	4.7	5.1	5.0	5.0	4.8	4.9
3. Difference between items 1 and 2:											
Nine consumer finance companies	1.7	1.7	1.6	1.7	1.6	1.6	1.5	1.5	1.6	1.3	1.3
Ten sales finance companies	1.4	1.4	1.3	1.2	1.1	1.1	.9	.9	1.0	.9	.9
Nine commercial banks	—	—	—	—	—	—	.6	.8	.9	.9	.9
All federal credit unions	.5	.6	.5	.6	.6	.6	.6	.5	.5	.5	.4
4. Nonearning assets as percentage of total assets											
Nine consumer finance companies	15.6	15.1	14.9	15.1	15.1	15.2	14.5	13.9	13.7	13.5	12.8
Ten sales finance companies	16.4	14.9	14.1	13.8	13.2	12.6	12.0	11.9	12.0	12.4	12.0
Nine commercial banks	—	—	—	—	—	—	22.4	23.6	23.7	22.6	22.9
All federal credit unions	11.4	10.9	12.3	11.9	10.2	9.9	9.5	8.8	8.5	8.5	7.8

a slight decline in the return on total assets and a sharp increase in the cost of nonequity funds. As shown in Chart 15, the net return on non-equity funds declined from 6.3 to 4.5 per cent from 1949 to 1959 at consumer finance companies and from 3.8 to 2.1 per cent at sales finance companies.

At the same time both types of company were able to increase the proportion of nonequity funds used in their lending operations. This enabled them to reduce the impact of the decline in net return on non-equity funds on profits. Nevertheless, the profit from the use of nonequity funds declined at both types of finance company. The decline was sharper at sales finance companies where the added income from lever-age in 1959 was only 70 per cent of that of the early 1950's. Consumer finance companies were able to hold their position somewhat better and showed a smaller decline in profits from this source.

During the five-year period from 1955 to 1959, the sample banks were able to improve their return on nonequity funds. This improvement resulted largely from a gain in net operating income on total assets and reflected primarily the increase in general market rates on noncon-sumer loans and investments. The gain in net return on nonequity funds was offset in part, however, by a slight decline in the ratio of non-equity funds to total funds. Their nonequity funds declined from eleven times net worth in 1955 to 9.6 times in 1959.

RATE OF PROFITS[1]

Finance companies faced a number of developments that reduced their return on equity funds during the 1950's: (1) a decline in their gross earn-ings on consumer credit; (2) a decline in net operating income from consumer credit; and (3) a sharp rise in the cost of nonequity funds. A number of favorable developments improving their profitability helped balance the unfavorable factors: They were able: (1) to maintain or increase their earnings on nonconsumer credit and other activities; (2) to reduce the cost of nonearning assets; and (3) to increase the use of nonequity funds. They were unable to stem the adverse developments on profits completely, however, and the rate of return on equity was smaller in the late 1950's than in the earlier part of the decade (Chart 16). The decline in the return on equity funds was most pronounced at the sample sales finance companies whose return declined to 10 per

---

[1] The term "net income" has been used to indicate the return after expenses for federal credit unions instead of net profits because of differences in the ownership and objectives of credit unions.

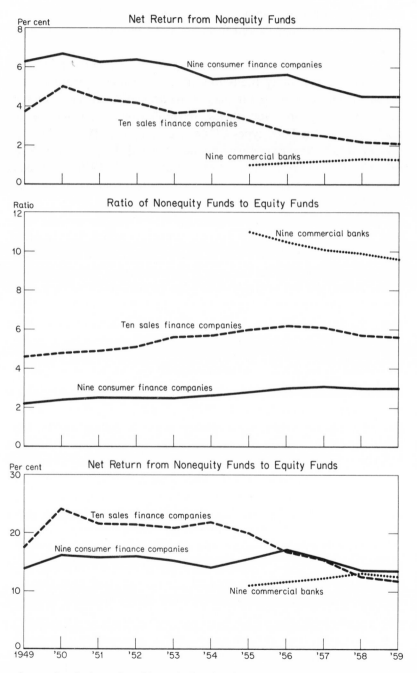

CHART 15

Financial Advantage of Use of Nonequity Funds, by Type of
Institution, 1949–59

Net Return from Nonequity Funds

Per cent

Nine consumer finance companies

Ten sales finance companies

Nine commercial banks

Ratio of Nonequity Funds to Equity Funds

Ratio

Nine commercial banks

Ten sales finance companies

Nine consumer finance companies

Net Return from Nonequity Funds to Equity Funds

Per cent

Ten sales finance companies

Nine consumer finance companies

Nine commercial banks

1949   '50   '51   '52   '53   '54   '55   '56   '57   '58   '59

SOURCE: Sample data collected for study. Based on data in Tables 6, 13, and 20.

CHART 16
Return on Equity Funds by Type of Institution, 1949–59

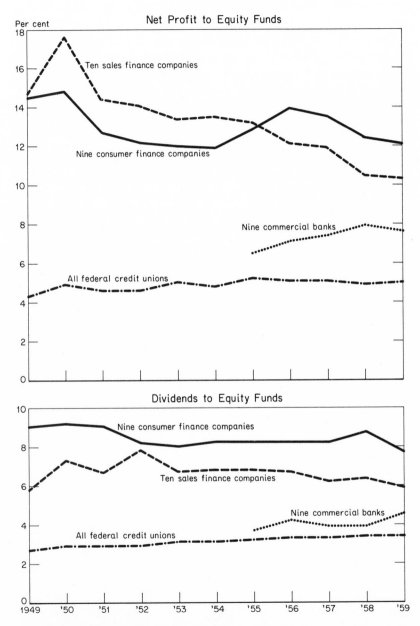

SOURCE: Bureau of Federal Credit Unions and sample data collected for study. Based on data in Appendix Tables B-5, C-5, D-5, and E-5.

cent on equity in 1958–59, compared with a return of about 15 per cent in the early 1950's and even higher rates in the mid-1930's.[2] Consumer finance companies showed only a slight decline in the rate earned on equity during the 1950's.

The net income of federal credit unions was relatively stable throughout the period. They were unaffected by many of the adverse factors affecting stockholder-owned institutions. Rising interest costs increased their return from nonconsumer investments and were of minor importance as a factor in higher costs because they made little use of nonequity funds. They also maintained relative stability in the gross earnings on their consumer credit receivables.

Commercial banks were able to improve their profits during the last five years of the 1950's. The increase in interest rates was more important as a source of additional profits than as a cost. They were able to increase their return on consumer credit and other earning assets and, despite some rise in the cost of funds, their net return on the use of nonequity funds increased in contrast to the experience of finance companies. They were able to increase their over-all return from nonequity funds even while expanding their proportion of equity funds.

The pattern of cash payment to owners differed widely among the four types of institutions (Chart 16). Consumer finance companies reduced their cash payments as a percentage of equity throughout the eleven-year period. Credit unions increased their payments as a percentage of equity funds, while sales finance companies and banks showed sizable year-to-year variations with no distinct trend.

[2] Ernst Dauer, *Comparative Operating Experience of Consumer Instalment Financing Agencies and Commercial Banks, 1929–41,* New York, NBER, 1944.

APPENDIX A
Description of Samples and Adjustments in Data

THE information used in the study was based on a variety of published and unpublished materials. Published financial statements for the sample companies were supplemented by data obtained from cooperating companies. Two types of adjustments had to be made in the information obtained from the sample companies. First, statement data had to be adjusted to conform to the conceptual framework used in the study. Second, estimates of selected items had to be made when the accounting records of the company could not provide the necessary detail.

All income and expense data for the sample companies were classified into three groups: (1) those associated with consumer credit activities, (2) those associated with all other earning activities, and (3) those associated with obtaining funds, either equity or nonequity. Cost accounting data were used to establish the proper classification except in a few cases where estimates had to be made.

The cost of funds, both equity and nonequity, and provision for income taxes were further allocated to consumer credit and other activities by the following rules: (1) The costs of nonequity funds were distributed according to the proportion of average earning assets used in these activities. (2) Income taxes and cost of equity funds were distributed according to the proportion of net operating income obtained from these activities. The details of the adjustments in individual company data are presented in the following discussion by type of institution.

The samples used in the study were necessarily small because only relatively few companies could supply the detail needed and because of the elaborate processing of the data that was required. The results of the study do not necessarily represent all companies operating in the industries covered but are intended merely to present data on costs in a standard accounting framework that will suggest differences in costs and operating problems by type of institution.

Consumer Finance Companies

The following consumer finance companies supplied the information used in the study:

> American Investment Company of Illinois
> Beneficial Finance Company
> Family Finance Corporation
> Household Finance Corporation

117

Interstate Finance Corporation
Liberty Loan Corporation
Merchants Acceptance Corporation
Seaboard Finance Company
State Loan & Finance Corporation

These nine companies held $2.3 billion in consumer receivables at the end of 1959 and accounted for 70 per cent of the loans held by all consumer finance companies. All of these companies are among the largest in operation. Together they had 4,356 branch offices and had a loan volume of over $3 billion in 1959. All but two of them had more than $100 million in receivables and all but one had more than 100 branch offices. A comparison of some of the principal characteristics of these companies with estimates for all consumer finance companies based on a survey conducted in 1955 is shown in Table A-1.

Although all of the companies in this group engaged primarily in making loans under the state small-loan law, a few of them held substantial amounts of purchased instalment contracts either secured by automobiles or other durable goods. Their other activities, limited primarily to insurance and wholesale financing of dealer inventories, represented a relatively small part of the total activities, when measured by either income received or funds invested.

Since the information available from the accounting records of these companies differed in form of presentation and in composition, some rearrangement in the data was necessary to obtain uniformity. Estimates were also necessary in some cases to fill gaps in accounting information. The following list describes the principal adjustments that were made in the data for some of these companies to adapt the information for use in the study. The procedures used in making these adjustments and estimating missing data necessarily varied from company to company depending upon circumstances.

1. Reserves for bad-debt losses were added to the outstanding amount of receivables in cases where they had been subtracted in the financial statements of the reporting companies. Total assets were increased accordingly and the amount of reserves was included in the equity of the company.

2. Unearned discount was included in gross receivables, but was deducted to obtain net figures and total assets.

3. The current portion of debentures and other long-term debt was removed from figures for short-term debt and was included with long-term debt.

TABLE A-1

COMPARISON OF CONSUMER FINANCE COMPANY SAMPLE WITH ESTIMATES FOR ALL COMPANIES, 1955

Item	All Consumer Finance Companies[a]		Nine Sample Companies[b]		Sample as Percentage of Total (5)	Differences in Percentage Distribution (col.4 minus col. 2) (6)
	Million Dollars (1)	Per Cent (2)	Million Dollars (3)	Per Cent (4)		
Number of companies:						
Total[c]	3,180		9		0.3	—
By size of consumer receivables outstanding (thousand dollars):						
25,000 and over	10		7		70.0	—
5,000 to 25,999	48		2		4.2	—
Under 5,000	3,120		0		0	—
Principal sources and uses of funds:						
Consumer receivables, total	2,398	82.9	1,320	91.1	55.0	8.2
Personal loans	1,977	68.4	1,189	82.1	60.1	13.7
Other consumer receivables	421	14.5	131	9.0	31.1	-5.5
Other earning assets	310	10.7	8	.5	2.6	-10.2
less						
Reserves for unearned income[d]	(148)	(5.1)	(35)	(2.4)	23.6	(-2.7)
Other assets	331	11.5	156	10.8	47.1	-.7
Total uses	2,891	100.0	1,449	100.0	50.1	—
Nonequity funds	2,035	70.4	1,026	70.8	50.4	.4
Equity funds[e]	856	29.6	423	29.2	49.4	-.4

a
Data as of June 30, 1955, based on survey of finance companies conducted by Board of Governors of Federal Reserve System, Federal Reserve Bulletin, April 1957, pp. 392-408.
b
Sources and uses of funds figures are averages for the beginning and end of 1955.
c
Number of companies for total and smallest size group rounded to nearest ten.
d
Survey data include reserves for losses.
e
Sample data include reserves for losses.

4. Estimates of the administrative costs of obtaining funds were made for each company on the basis of cost studies available for one company. The amount of these costs was deducted from operating cost and included with the cost of nonequity funds.

5. Where free life insurance was extended to borrowers, the cost of this insurance was deducted from gross income and from expenses.

6. Estimates of the cost of insurance operations were made for companies that did not have separate insurance subsidiaries and could not provide separate cost figures. These costs were included in the nonconsumer credit operating costs.

7. Estimates of the cost of wholesale financing were made on the basis of cost data from sales finance companies. These costs were included as nonconsumer credit operating expenses.

Sales Finance Companies

The following sales finance companies supplied the information used in the study:

> American Discount Company
> Associate Investment Company
> C.I.T. Financial Corporation
> General Acceptance Corporation
> General Finance Corporation
> General Motors Acceptance Corporation
> Interstate Securities Company
> Pacific Finance Corporation
> Securities Acceptance Corporation
> Southwestern Investment Company

All of these companies are among the largest companies engaged in automobile financing. Together they held $5.8 billion in automobile paper at the end of 1959, or 83 per cent of the automobile paper held by all sales finance companies. All of the sample companies had $35 million or more in automobile paper at the end of 1959 and all of them operated in many states.

A comparison of the sample with estimates for all sales finance companies for 1955 is shown in Table A-2. Although the sample companies represented only .4 per cent of the total number of companies, they held 76 per cent of the automobile paper and 45 per cent of the personal loans of all sales finance companies. Since the sample was selected on

TABLE A-2

COMPARISON OF SALES FINANCE COMPANY SAMPLE WITH ESTIMATES FOR ALL COMPANIES, 1955

Item	All Sales Finance Companies[a]		Ten Sample Companies[b]		Sample as Percentage of Total (5)	Differences in Percentage Distribution (col. 4 minus col. 2) (6)
	Million Dollars (1)	Per Cent (2)	Million Dollars (3)	Per Cent (4)		
Number of companies:						
Total[c]	2,620		10		0.4	—
By size of consumer receivables outstanding (thousand dollars):						
25,000 and over	20		10		50.0	—
5,000 to 24,999	61		0		0	—
Under 5,000	2,540		0		0	—
Principal sources and uses of funds:						
Consumer receivables, total	7,317	72.6	4,926	75.9	67.3	3.3
Automobile paper	5,976	59.3	4,563	70.4	76.4	11.1
Other consumer goods paper	920	9.1	173	2.6	18.8	-6.5
Personal loans	421	4.2	190	2.9	45.1	-1.3
Other earning assets	2,684	26.6	1,485	22.9	55.3	-3.7
less Reserves for unearned income[d]	(795)	(7.9)	(350)	(5.4)	44.0	(2.5)
Other assets	871	8.7	425	6.6	53.5	-2.1
Total uses	10,077	100.0	6,486	100.0	64.4	—
Nonequity funds	8,579	85.1	5,773	89.0	67.3	3.9
Equity funds[e]	1,498	14.9	713	11.0	47.6	-3.9

a
Data as of June 30, 1955, based on survey of finance companies conducted by Board of Governors of Federal Reserve System, Federal Reserve Bulletin, April 1957, pp. 392-408.

b
Sources and uses of funds figures are averages for beginning and end of 1955.

c
Number of companies for total and smallest size group rounded to nearest ten.

d
Survey data also include reserves for losses.   eSample data include reserves for losses.

the basis of automobile financing, they held a somewhat smaller share of total appliance and other consumer goods paper.

The companies in this sample showed a wider variety of other earning assets than the consumer finance companies. All of the companies in this sample did some wholesale financing of dealer inventories and most of them had insurance subsidiaries. In addition, many of them made capital loans to automobile dealers or other retailers and a few of them engaged in a sizable amount of equipment financing or other forms of business financing. When the nonconsumer credit operations were handled by separate subsidiaries, income and expense figures could be easily separated from consumer credit operations. In other cases, estimates had to be prepared of the costs of the nonconsumer credit activities. These were based on information available from companies that had cost information on the various types of activities. Where truck or commercial vehicle financing could not be segregated from automobile financing, no attempt was made to prepare separate cost estimates or to eliminate truck or commercial vehicle receivables from the receivables included in the consumer total. It was felt that the errors involved in such estimates might result in a larger distortion of the financial ratios than the inclusion of data for these activities in the consumer credit totals.

The other adjustments made in data supplied by sales finance companies were similar to those described for consumer finance companies in the preceding section.

Commercial Banks

The following commercial banks submitted information for use in the study:

Bankers Trust Company, New York, N.Y.
Bank of America NT & SA, San Francisco, Calif.
City National Bank & Trust Co., Kansas City, Mo.
First National Bank of Boston, Mass.
First National City Bank, New York, N.Y.
First Pennsylvania Banking & Trust Co., Phila., Pa.
Marine Trust Company of Western New York, Buffalo, N.Y.
National Shawmut Bank, Boston, Mass.
Pittsburgh National Bank, Pittsburgh, Pa.
Provident Tradesmen's Bank & Trust, Phila., Pa.
Security First National Bank, Los Angeles, Calif.

United California Bank, Los Angeles, Calif.
Valley National Bank, Phoenix, Arizona
Wells Fargo Bank American Trust Company, San Francisco, Calif.

Since commercial bank activities are widely diversified, only a few banks with extensive cost accounting systems were able to provide estimates of the cost of their consumer credit operations. Even the information that can be obtained differs greatly in concept and coverage. Some estimates are based on the costs of the consumer credit department plus a share of the bank's overhead costs (indirect costs). Only a few banks make estimates of the cost of branch personnel in accepting consumer loan applications and in receiving payments.

All of the information from the cooperating banks could not be used in the tabulations required for the study because of differences in accounting concepts and practices. The main financial ratios used were based on data from nine of the cooperating banks that were able to provide the required detail and that had reasonably comparable accounting systems. A somewhat different grouping of banks was used in supplementary tabulations to develop as much information as possible on the nature of costs by type of consumer credit.

Table A-3 compares the nine sample banks with data for all commercial banks at the end of 1959. The nine sample banks held 7 per cent of the consumer loans of all commercial banks, although they represented only six one-hundredths of the total number of banks.

Although all the banks in the sample had sizable instalment loan operations, their operations accounted for a relatively small fraction of

TABLE A-3

COMPARISON OF COMMERCIAL BANK SAMPLE WITH DATA
FOR ALL COMMERCIAL BANKS, END OF 1959
(million dollars)

Item	All Commercial Banks	Nine-Bank Sample	Sample as Percentage of Total
Number of banks	13,991	9	.06
Total loans and investments	227,831	15,295	6.71
Consumer credit	15,227	1,041	6.84
Total deposits	254,885	17,738	7.00

their total loans and investments. Consumer credit of the sample average only 8 per cent of total earning assets and ranged from 2 per cent at one bank to 18 per cent at another.

All but one of the banks included in the nine-bank sample had extensive branch operations. Most of them were engaged in all major types of consumer lending, although the importance of various types of credit varied from bank to bank. Automobile paper, both direct and indirect, was the most important type of consumer receivable at three of the sample banks, personal loans were most important at four banks, and other consumer goods paper accounted for the largest percentage of consumer credit at one bank.

The information prepared for the study differs in a number of ways from the banking statements prepared for supervisory agencies and published in annual reports. Numerous adjustments and estimates were made in data obtained from cooperating banks to develop information needed in the study. The procedures used for making adjustments in individual bank data differed from bank to bank. The principal adjustments necessary in reported data were as follows:

1. Unearned income was deducted from the outstanding amount of loans and from "other liabilities." The amount of unearned income is shown separately but total assets are net of this amount.

2. The asset item "customer's liability on acceptances outstanding" was subtracted from the liability item "acceptances executed by or for account of this bank and outstanding." Only the net balance of these accounts was included in total assets.

3. Valuation reserves on loans were added to the outstanding amount of loans and total assets. The amount of these reserves was included in equity funds.

4. Estimates of the operating cost of consumer credit had to be adjusted or modified in a number of cases to make estimates from different banks conceptually comparable.

5. When estimates of cost of handling deposits were based on a single survey, projections of these costs had to be made for other years covered by the study.

6. Total deposits were reduced by the amount of dealer reserves. Dealer reserve accounts are shown separately.

Federal Credit Unions

Information used for federal credit unions was based on tabulations published annually by the Bureau of Federal Credit Unions. The figures

TABLE A-4

ADJUSTMENTS IN PUBLISHED DATA FOR FEDERAL CREDIT UNIONS, 1959
(thousand dollars)

Item	Published Data[a]	Adjust-ments[a]	Data Used in Study
Gross income	171,847		158,015
Interest on loans	152,909		139,077
minus			
Borrower protection insurance		−8,577	
Interest refunds		−5,255[b]	
Other income	18,938		18,938
Expenses	69,610		50,304
minus			
Borrower protection insurance		−8,577	
Life savings insurance		−5,784	
Estimate of cost of handling share accounts		−8,976[c]	
Interest on borrowed money		−1,799	
plus			
Losses on loans		+5,830[d]	
Net income	102,237		
Net operating income	--		107,709
Cost of nonequity funds			1,799
Cost of equity funds (net income)			105,910
Benefits, life savings insurance			5,784
Benefits, handling of share accounts			8,976[c]
Return on equity funds			91,150

a
As published in 1959 Report of Operations, Federal Credit Unions, U.S. Department of Health, Education, and Welfare, pp. 24–25.
b
Ibid., p. 28.
c
Based on costs of handling time deposits at commercial banks with allowances for differentials in costs at commercial banks and credit unions.
d
Obtained by subtracting "losses charged off from date of organization through December 31, 1958" (Table 24, 1958 Report of Operations) from same item in 1959 Report of Operations (Table 24, p. 30).

used in the study were aggregates for all federal credit unions. In 1959 the data covered 9,447 credit unions with consumer loans of $1,666 million.

Details on many aspects of credit union operations are published in the annual reports of the Bureau of Federal Credit Unions and are not reproduced in this study. These institutions ranged from newly formed organizations with only a few thousand dollars in assets to multimillion-dollar organizations.

The absolute dollar range in these organizations is much smaller than that for finance companies or banks because of the existence of billion-dollar banks and finance companies. As a result, finance ratios based on averages of aggregate figures are more representative of the average credit union than aggregate ratios for finance companies would be.

Several adjustments were made in the published income and expense data to bring them into the conceptual framework used in the study. Table A-4 shows a reconciliation of the published figures with the figures used in computing the ratios for the study and indicates the nature and extent of the adjustment of the original data. Since losses on loans are not published separately in the federal credit union report, these figures had to be derived from cumulative figures on losses published each year. The figure used in the study was obtained by subtracting the figures for the preceding year from the total for the year in question.

APPENDIX B

Supplementary Tabulations for Consumer Finance Companies

TABLE B-1

DISTRIBUTION OF SOURCES AND USES OF FUNDS OF CONSUMER FINANCE COMPANIES, END OF YEAR, 1948–59
(per cent)

Item	1948	1949	1950	1951	1952	1953	1954	1955	1956	1957	1958	1959
Sources of funds:												
Debt, total	63.3	63.1	65.7	65.2	64.2	65.1	66.9	69.0	70.6	70.4	69.4	70.8
Short-term to banks	40.0	37.1	39.3	33.3	33.2	33.8	27.8	35.2	31.1	28.0	26.0	26.2
Other short-term[a]	6.0	7.1	5.5	5.9	7.2	5.9	7.9	4.8	4.9	4.4	5.2	7.1
Senior long-term	10.1	11.0	12.9	19.4	17.8	19.2	22.3	20.5	26.3	29.1	29.2	28.3
Subordinated	7.2	7.9	8.0	6.6	6.0	6.2	8.9	8.5	8.3	8.9	9.0	9.2
Dealer reserves	0.2	0.2	0.2	0.2	0.2	0.3	0.4	0.4	0.4	0.3	0.3	0.3
Other liabilities	4.1	4.3	4.6	5.3	6.0	5.7	5.1	4.6	4.5	4.3	4.1	4.1
Total nonequity funds	67.6	67.6	70.5	70.7	70.4	71.1	72.4	74.0	75.5	75.0	73.8	75.2
Equity funds, total	32.4	32.4	29.5	29.3	29.6	28.9	27.6	26.0	24.5	25.0	26.2	24.8
Reserves	3.4	3.2	3.2	3.1	3.1	3.2	3.2	3.1	3.1	3.1.	3.2	3.2
Preferred stock	10.6	10.6	7.4	7.8	8.6	7.0	5.1	3.9	3.3	4.2	4.3	3.7
Common stock and surplus	18.4	18.6	18.9	18.4	17.9	18.7	19.3	19.0	18.1	17.7	18.7	17.9
Total	100.0	100.0	100.0	100.0	100.0	100.0	100.0	100.0	100.0	100.0	100.0	100.0

(continued)

TABLE B-1 (concluded)

Item	1948	1949	1950	1951	1952	1953	1954	1955	1956	1957	1958	1959
Uses of funds:												
Earning assets, gross	86.1	87.3	87.9	88.4	88.3	88.8	88.1	90.3	90.8	92.2	92.5	94.6
Consumer credit	84.4	85.5	85.5	86.2	86.8	87.4	86.9	88.9	89.8	91.1	91.2	93.4
Other	1.7	1.8	2.4	2.2	1.5	1.4	1.2	1.4	1.0	1.1	1.3	1.2
less Unearned income[b]	2.7	2.5	2.9	3.2	3.6	3.7	3.5	4.1	4.7	5.7	6.1	6.9
Earning assets, net	83.4	84.8	85.0	85.2	84.7	85.1	84.6	86.2	86.1	86.5	86.4	87.7
Consumer credit	81.7	83.0	82.6	83.0	83.2	83.7	83.4	84.8	85.1	85.4	85.1	86.5
Automobile paper	4.3	4.3	5.1	4.7	3.3	4.0	3.4	3.6	3.0	1.6	1.2	1.8
Other goods paper	5.2	4.9	5.7	5.4	5.3	5.4	5.6	6.7	7.1	6.5	5.9	6.8
Personal loans	72.2	73.8	71.8	72.9	74.6	74.3	74.4	74.5	75.0	77.3	78.0	77.9
Other	1.7	1.8	2.4	2.2	1.5	1.4	1.2	1.4	1.0	1.1	1.3	1.2
Cash and bank balances	12.8	12.1	11.6	11.2	11.7	11.6	11.6	10.1	10.2	9.8	10.0	9.0
Other assets	3.8	3.1	3.4	3.6	3.6	3.3	3.8	3.7	3.7	3.7	3.6	3.3
Total	100.0	100.0	100.0	100.0	100.0	100.0	100.0	100.0	100.0	100.0	100.0	100.0

Source: All data are averages of ratios for nine sample companies. See Appendix A for a description of the sample and of the processing of the data. Detail may not add to totals because of rounding.

[a] Includes small amounts of certificates of deposit and thrift accounts of employees.
[b] On consumer assets only.

TABLE B-2

DISTRIBUTION OF SOURCES AND USES OF FUNDS OF CONSUMER FINANCE COMPANIES, AVERAGES OF
BEGINNING AND END OF YEAR, 1949-59
(per cent)

Item	1949	1950	1951	1952	1953	1954	1955	1956	1957	1958	1959
Sources of funds:											
Debt, total	62.8	64.7	65.4	64.6	64.7	66.1	68.1	70.0	70.5	69.9	70.2
Short-term to banks	37.9	38.6	36.0	33.2	33.5	30.6	31.8	32.9	29.3	27.1	26.2
Other short-term	6.8	6.2	5.7	6.6	6.5	7.0	6.3	4.9	4.6	4.8	6.4
Senior long-term	10.7	12.0	16.5	18.5	18.6	20.8	21.3	23.7	27.8	29.1	28.5
Subordinated	7.4	7.9	7.2	6.3	6.1	7.7	8.7	8.4	8.8	8.9	9.1
Dealer reserve	.2	.2	.2	.2	.3	.3	.4	.4	.3	.3	.3
Other liabilities	4.0	4.6	5.1	5.7	5.8	5.4	4.8	4.5	4.4	4.2	4.1
Total nonequity funds	67.0	69.5	70.7	70.5	70.8	71.8	73.3	74.8	75.2	74.4	74.6
Equity funds, total	33.0	30.5	29.2	29.5	29.2	28.2	26.7	25.2	24.8	25.6	25.4
Reserves	3.3	3.1	3.1	3.1	3.1	3.2	3.1	3.1	3.1	3.2	3.2
Preferred stock	10.8	8.8	7.7	8.3	7.8	6.0	4.5	3.6	3.8	4.2	4.0
Common stock and surplus	18.9	18.6	18.5	18.1	18.3	19.0	19.1	18.5	17.9	18.2	18.2
Total	100.0	100.0	100.0	100.0	100.0	100.0	100.0	100.0	100.0	100.0	100.0

(continued)

TABLE B-2 (concluded)

Item	1949	1950	1951	1952	1953	1954	1955	1956	1957	1958	1959
Uses of funds:											
Earning assets, gross	86.8	87.7	88.2	88.3	88.5	88.4	89.3	90.6	91.5	92.3	93.6
Consumer credit	85.1	85.5	85.9	86.5	87.1	87.1	88.0	89.4	90.5	91.2	92.4
Other	1.7	2.2	2.3	1.8	1.4	1.3	1.3	1.2	1.0	1.1	1.2
less											
Unearned income[a]	2.4	2.8	3.1	3.4	3.6	3.6	3.8	4.5	5.2	5.8	6.4
Earning assets, net	84.4	84.9	85.1	84.9	84.9	84.8	85.5	86.1	86.3	86.5	87.2
Consumer credit	82.6	82.7	82.8	83.1	83.5	83.5	84.2	84.9	85.3	85.3	85.9
Automobile paper	3.8	4.9	4.7	3.7	3.4	3.5	3.2	3.1	2.1	1.4	1.6
Other goods paper	3.5	5.1	5.4	5.3	5.3	5.3	6.0	6.7	6.7	6.1	6.3
Personal loans	75.3	72.7	72.7	74.1	74.8	74.7	75.0	75.1	76.5	77.8	78.0
Other	1.8	2.2	2.3	1.8	1.4	1.3	1.3	1.2	1.0	1.2	1.3
Cash and bank balances	12.2	11.8	11.4	11.5	11.7	11.6	10.8	10.2	10.0	9.9	9.4
Other assets	3.4	3.3	3.5	3.6	3.4	3.6	3.7	3.7	3.7	3.6	3.4
Total	100.0	100.0	100.0	100.0	100.0	100.0	100.0	100.0	100.0	100.0	100.0

Source: See source to Table B-1.

[a]On consumer assets only.

TABLE B-3

DISTRIBUTION OF EARNINGS AND EXPENSES OF CONSUMER FINANCE COMPANIES, 1949–59

(per cent)

Item	1949	1950	1951	1952	1953	1954	1955	1956	1957	1958	1959
Earnings	100.0	100.0	100.0	100.0	100.0	100.0	100.0	100.0	100.0	100.0	100.0
Consumer credit	96.8	96.2	95.3	95.2	95.3	94.9	93.7	93.8	93.7	94.8	93.7
Other	3.2	3.8	4.7	4.8	4.7	5.1	6.3	6.2	6.3	5.2	6.3
Operating expenses	58.9	56.8	57.2	56.3	56.6	58.2	58.8	56.5	56.9	59.4	58.3
Consumer credit	58.4	55.7	55.5	54.6	54.6	55.8	55.9	53.8	54.1	56.6	55.4
Other	.5	1.1	1.7	1.7	2.0	2.4	2.9	2.7	2.8	2.8	2.9
Net operating income	41.1	43.2	42.8	43.7	43.4	41.8	41.2	43.5	43.1	40.6	41.7
Consumer credit	38.3	40.5	39.8	40.6	40.6	39.1	37.7	40.0	39.7	37.1	38.4
Other	2.8	2.7	3.0	3.1	2.8	2.7	3.5	3.5	3.4	3.5	3.3
Cost of funds	8.8	8.8	9.7	10.6	11.3	11.9	11.8	13.5	14.9	15.0	15.8
Consumer credit	8.6	8.6	9.5	10.4	11.1	11.7	11.6	13.3	14.7	14.8	15.5
Other	.2	.2	.2	.2	.2	.2	.2	.2	.2	.2	.3
Net profit before taxes	32.3	34.4	33.1	33.1	32.1	29.9	29.4	30.0	28.2	25.6	25.9
Consumer credit	29.8	31.9	30.3	30.2	29.5	27.4	26.2	26.7	25.0	22.3	22.7
Other	2.5	2.5	2.8	2.9	2.6	2.5	3.2	3.3	3.2	3.3	3.2
Provision for income tax	11.9	14.3	16.2	17.3	16.4	14.5	13.8	14.1	12.9	11.1	11.8
Consumer credit	11.2	13.5	15.2	16.1	15.4	13.7	12.9	13.1	12.1	10.3	10.9
Other	.7	.8	1.0	1.2	1.0	.8	.9	1.0	.8	.8	.9
Net profit	20.4	20.1	16.9	15.8	15.7	15.4	15.6	15.9	15.3	14.5	14.1
Consumer credit	18.5	18.4	15.1	14.1	14.1	13.7	13.3	13.6	12.9	12.0	11.8
Other	1.9	1.7	1.8	1.7	1.6	1.7	2.3	2.3	2.4	2.5	2.3
Dividends	12.6	12.4	11.9	10.6	10.4	10.6	9.9	9.4	9.2	10.1	8.9
Preferred	2.3	2.0	1.7	2.0	1.8	1.4	1.0	.8	.9	1.0	.9
Common	10.3	10.4	10.2	8.6	8.6	9.2	8.9	8.6	8.3	9.1	8.0

Source: See source to Table B-1.

TABLE B-4

COMPONENTS OF GROSS FINANCE CHARGES ON CONSUMER CREDIT AT CONSUMER FINANCE COMPANIES, 1949-59

(dollars per $100 of average outstanding consumer credit)

Item	1949	1950	1951	1952	1953	1954	1955	1956	1957	1958	1959
Gross finance charges[a]	26.06	25.75	25.31	25.99	25.47	24.41	24.17	24.28	24.13	24.21	24.04
Dealer's share of gross finance charges	.09	.20	.17	.18	.18	.18	.17	.17	.17	.18	.17
Lender's gross revenue	25.97	25.55	25.14	25.81	25.29	24.23	24.00	24.11	23.96	24.03	23.87
Operating expenses	15.72	14.87	14.77	14.94	14.66	14.36	14.46	13.94	13.93	14.64	14.25
Salaries	7.12	6.70	6.79	6.91	6.82	6.57	6.65	6.47	6.40	6.69	6.45
Occupancy costs	1.21	1.08	1.07	1.08	1.08	1.05	1.07	1.05	1.03	1.10	1.09
Advertising	1.38	1.25	1.24	1.14	1.03	.87	.97	.93	.85	.80	.89
Provision for losses	2.03	2.13	1.88	1.86	1.81	1.79	1.84	1.70	1.72	2.02	1.98
Actual losses[b]	(1.47)	(1.42)	(1.51)	(1.38)	(1.43)	(1.50)	(1.39)	(1.15)	(1.39)	(1.71)	(1.70)
Other	3.98	3.71	3.79	3.95	3.92	4.08	3.93	3.79	3.93	4.03	3.84
Nonoperating expenses	10.25	10.68	10.37	10.87	10.63	9.87	9.54	10.17	10.03	9.39	9.62
Cost of nonequity funds	2.29	2.28	2.50	2.81	2.93	2.98	2.97	3.41	3.77	3.80	3.97
Income taxes	2.99	3.54	3.95	4.30	4.03	3.42	3.22	3.30	3.01	2.56	2.73
Cost of equity funds (lender's profit)	4.97	4.86	3.92	3.76	3.67	3.47	3.35	3.46	3.25	3.03	2.92
Retained	1.62	1.61	.81	.88	.92	.76	.81	1.03	.87	.35	.61
Dividends	3.35	3.25	3.11	2.88	2.75	2.71	2.54	2.43	2.38	2.68	2.31

Source: See source to Table B-1.

a
Includes all finance charges and fees collected on consumer credit activities. Charges for insurance are not included and the cost of free insurance provided to borrowers was deducted.

b
Net of recoveries.

TABLE B-5

SELECTED RATIOS FOR CONSUMER FINANCE COMPANIES, 1949-59
(per cent)

	1949	1950	1951	1952	1953	1954	1955	1956	1957	1958	1959
Ratios to total assets of:											
Earnings	22.2	22.0	21.7	22.4	22.0	21.3	21.6	21.8	21.7	21.8	21.8
Operating expenses	13.1	12.5	12.4	12.6	12.4	12.4	12.7	12.3	12.4	12.9	12.7
Net operating income	9.1	9.5	9.3	9.8	9.6	8.9	8.9	9.5	9.3	8.9	9.1
Cost of funds	1.9	1.9	2.1	2.4	2.5	2.5	2.5	2.9	3.2	3.3	3.4
Net profit before taxes	7.2	7.6	7.2	7.4	7.1	6.4	6.4	6.6	6.1	5.6	5.7
Provision for income taxes	2.7	3.2	3.5	3.9	3.6	3.1	3.0	3.1	2.8	2.4	2.6
Net profits	4.5	4.4	3.7	3.5	3.5	3.3	3.4	3.5	3.3	3.2	3.1
Ratios to equity funds of:											
Net profits before taxes	23.1	25.3	24.9	25.5	24.4	23.0	24.2	26.2	24.9	21.9	22.2
Net profits	14.5	14.8	12.7	12.2	12.0	11.9	12.8	13.9	13.5	12.4	12.1
Dividends	9.0	9.2	9.0	8.2	8.0	8.2	8.2	8.2	8.2	8.7	7.7
Ratios of earnings to earning assets:											
Total earnings	26.3	25.9	25.7	26.5	26.1	25.2	25.3	25.4	25.3	25.4	25.1
Consumer credit earnings	26.0	25.6	25.1	25.8	25.3	24.2	24.0	24.1	24.0	24.0	23.9
Personal loan earnings	27.5	27.5	27.4	27.4	27.0	25.7	25.6	25.6	25.1	25.1	24.9
Ratios of cost of nonequity funds to:											
Total debt	3.0	3.0	3.2	3.7	3.8	3.8	3.7	4.2	4.6	4.7	5.0
Total nonequity funds	2.8	2.8	3.0	3.4	3.5	3.5	3.4	3.9	4.3	4.4	4.6

Source: See source to Table B-1.

APPENDIX C

Supplementary Tabulations for
Sales Finance Companies

TABLE C-1

DISTRIBUTION OF SOURCES AND USES OF FUNDS OF SALES FINANCE COMPANIES, END OF YEAR, 1948-59
(per cent)

Item	1948	1949	1950	1951	1952	1953	1954	1955	1956	1957	1958	1959
Sources of funds:												
Debt, total	70.8	70.3	70.5	71.6	73.1	75.4	74.2	77.4	77.3	78.0	76.6	78.5
Short-term to banks	49.5	43.5	45.0	45.2	43.7	40.0	35.4	40.0	34.3	34.9	28.3	29.8
Other short-term	9.4	11.2	9.1	10.7	12.8	12.2	13.7	9.6	10.9	11.3	15.4	16.6
Senior long-term	7.9	7.4	8.4	8.7	8.0	13.7	15.1	17.7	21.6	21.5	22.0	21.0
Subordinated	4.0	8.2	8.0	7.0	8.6	9.5	10.0	10.1	10.5	10.3	10.9	11.1
Dealer reserves	1.7	2.6	2.5	2.3	2.4	2.3	2.4	2.2	2.1	2.0	1.9	1.8
Other liabilities	10.4	8.3	8.8	8.0	7.8	6.1	6.7	5.8	5.3	4.8	4.8	4.6
Total nonequity funds	82.9	81.2	81.8	81.9	83.3	83.8	83.3	85.4	84.7	84.8	83.3	84.9
Equity funds, total	17.1	18.8	18.2	18.1	16.7	16.2	16.7	14.6	15.3	15.2	16.7	15.1
Reserves	2.5	2.3	2.5	2.8	2.7	2.5	2.4	2.3	2.3	2.3	2.1	2.0
Preferred stock	2.3	3.7	4.3	3.6	2.4	2.2	2.2	2.7	3.1	2.9	3.4	2.7
Common stock and surplus	12.3	12.8	11.4	11.7	11.6	11.5	12.1	9.6	9.9	10.0	11.2	10.4
Total	100.0	100.0	100.0	100.0	100.0	100.0	100.0	100.0	100.0	100.0	100.0	100.0

(continued)

TABLE C-1 (concluded)

Item	1948	1949	1950	1951	1952	1953	1954	1955	1956	1957	1958	1959
Uses of funds:												
Earning assets, gross	87.1	88.4	91.1	90.4	92.0	92.6	93.2	94.1	94.1	94.5	93.5	95.3
Consumer credit	65.6	71.6	74.4	72.2	76.9	77.4	79.6	79.6	80.4	78.5	77.2	78.3
Other	21.5	16.8	16.7	18.2	15.1	15.2	13.6	14.5	13.7	16.0	16.3	17.0
less												
Unearned income												
Consumer credit	3.5	4.7	5.0	4.6	5.6	5.4	5.7	5.9	6.2	6.4	6.4	6.7
Other	3.4	4.7	5.0	4.5	5.4	5.3	5.5	5.7	6.0	6.2	6.1	6.3
Other	.1	.1	.1	.1	.1	.1	.2	.2	.2	.2	.3	.4
Earning assets, net	83.6	83.7	86.1	85.8	86.4	87.2	87.5	88.2	87.9	88.1	87.1	88.6
Consumer credit	62.3	67.0	69.4	67.8	71.4	72.1	74.1	73.9	74.5	72.3	71.2	72.0
Automobile paper	51.7	55.0	58.2	54.9	57.8	57.8	59.4	60.7	59.2	55.0	51.5	52.9
Other goods paper	2.9	1.3	1.4	1.8	2.0	2.0	1.7	1.8	2.2	2.2	2.1	2.3
Personal loans	7.7	10.7	9.8	11.1	11.6	12.3	13.0	11.4	13.1	15.1	17.6	16.8
Other	21.3	16.7	16.7	18.0	15.0	15.1	13.4	14.3	13.4	15.8	15.9	16.6
Cash and bank balances	14.9	14.2	12.6	12.5	12.2	11.3	11.0	10.4	10.6	10.4	11.3	9.9
Other assets	1.5	2.1	1.3	1.7	1.4	1.5	1.5	1.4	1.5	1.5	1.6	1.5
Total	100.0	100.0	100.0	100.0	100.0	100.0	100.0	100.0	100.0	100.0	100.0	100.0

Source: All data are averages of ratios for ten sample companies. See Appendix A for a description of the sample and of the processing of the data. Detail may not add to totals because of rounding.

TABLE C-2

DISTRIBUTION OF SOURCES AND USES OF FUNDS OF SALES FINANCE COMPANIES, AVERAGES OF
BEGINNING AND END OF YEAR, 1949–59

(per cent)

Item	1949	1950	1951	1952	1953	1954	1955	1956	1957	1958	1959
Sources of funds:											
Debt, total	70.4	70.4	71.1	72.5	74.4	74.8	76.1	77.3	77.7	77.4	77.7
Short-term to banks	45.3	44.4	45.2	44.4	41.7	37.6	38.2	37.1	34.6	31.6	29.2
Other short-term	11.1	10.0	9.9	11.9	12.4	13.0	11.3	10.2	11.1	13.4	16.0
Senior long-term	6.9	8.0	8.6	8.3	11.2	14.5	16.6	19.7	21.6	21.8	21.5
Subordinated	7.1	8.0	7.4	7.9	9.1	9.7	10.0	10.3	10.4	10.6	11.0
Dealer reserves	2.5	2.5	2.4	2.3	2.3	2.4	2.3	2.2	2.0	2.0	1.8
Other liabilities	8.5	8.6	8.4	7.9	6.9	6.4	6.2	5.6	5.1	4.8	4.7
Total nonequity funds	81.4	81.5	81.9	82.7	83.6	83.6	84.6	85.1	84.8	84.2	84.2
Equity funds, total	18.6	18.5	18.1	17.3	16.4	16.4	15.4	14.9	15.2	15.8	15.8
Reserves	2.2	2.4	2.7	2.7	2.6	2.4	2.3	2.3	2.3	2.2	2.1
Preferred stock	3.7	4.1	3.9	3.0	2.3	2.2	2.5	2.9	3.0	3.1	3.0
Common stock and surplus	12.7	12.0	11.5	11.6	11.5	11.8	10.6	9.7	9.9	10.5	10.7
Total	100.0	100.0	100.0	100.0	100.0	100.0	100.0	100.0	100.0	100.0	100.0

(continued)

138

TABLE C-2 (concluded)

Item	1949	1950	1951	1952	1953	1954	1955	1956	1957	1958	1959
Uses of funds:											
Earning assets, gross	88.3	90.0	90.7	91.3	92.3	92.9	93.7	94.1	94.3	94.0	94.5
Consumer credit	70.6	73.2	73.2	74.8	77.1	78.5	79.6	80.1	79.4	77.9	77.9
Other	17.7	16.8	17.5	16.5	15.2	14.4	14.1	14.0	14.9	16.1	16.6
less											
Unearned income	4.7	4.9	4.8	5.1	5.5	5.5	5.7	6.0	6.3	6.4	6.5
Consumer credit	4.6	4.8	4.7	5.0	5.3	5.4	5.6	5.8	6.1	6.1	6.2
Other	.1	.1	.1	.1	.2	.1	.1	.2	.2	.3	.3
Earning assets, net	83.6	85.1	85.9	86.2	86.8	87.4	88.0	88.1	88.0	87.6	88.0
Consumer credit	66.0	68.3	68.5	69.8	71.8	73.1	74.0	74.2	73.3	71.7	71.7
Automobile paper	54.8	56.8	56.4	56.5	57.9	58.7	60.2	60.0	56.9	53.3	52.3
Other goods paper	1.4	1.4	1.6	1.9	1.9	1.8	1.8	2.0	2.2	2.1	2.2
Personal loans	9.8	10.1	10.5	11.4	12.0	12.6	12.0	12.2	14.2	16.3	17.2
Other	17.6	16.8	17.4	16.4	15.0	14.3	14.0	13.9	14.7	15.9	16.3
Cash and bank balances	14.3	13.3	12.6	12.3	11.7	11.1	10.6	10.5	10.5	10.8	10.5
Other assets	2.1	1.6	1.5	1.5	1.5	1.5	1.4	1.4	1.5	1.6	1.5
Total	100.0	100.0	100.0	100.0	100.0	100.0	100.0	100.0	100.0	100.0	100.0

Source: See source to Table C-1.

139

TABLE C-3

DISTRIBUTION OF EARNINGS AND EXPENSES OF SALES FINANCE COMPANIES, 1949–59
(per cent)

Item	1949	1950	1951	1952	1953	1954	1955	1956	1957	1958	1959
Earnings	100.0	100.0	100.0	100.0	100.0	100.0	100.0	100.0	100.0	100.0	100.0
Consumer credit	70.3	68.9	68.4	71.1	70.3	68.9	70.6	73.0	74.4	76.0	73.7
Other	29.7	31.1	31.6	28.9	29.7	31.1	29.4	27.0	25.6	24.0	26.3
Operating expenses	55.6	51.0	50.8	52.1	51.2	51.3	51.9	50.1	49.1	52.5	51.5
Consumer credit	40.3	34.2	32.6	35.3	37.7	38.3	38.7	37.6	37.3	42.6	41.0
Other	15.3	16.8	18.2	16.8	13.5	13.0	13.2	12.5	11.8	9.9	10.5
Net operating income	44.4	49.0	49.2	47.9	48.8	48.7	48.1	49.9	50.9	47.5	48.5
Consumer credit	30.0	34.7	35.8	35.8	32.7	30.6	32.0	35.5	37.1	33.5	32.8
Other	14.4	14.3	13.4	12.1	16.1	18.1	16.1	14.4	13.8	14.0	15.7
Cost of funds	14.6	13.7	16.0	17.1	20.0	19.5	20.4	24.8	26.9	25.7	27.3
Consumer credit	11.6	11.1	12.8	13.8	16.5	16.2	16.9	20.6	22.1	20.9	22.3
Other	3.0	2.6	3.2	3.3	3.5	3.3	3.5	4.2	4.8	4.8	5.0
Net profit before taxes	29.8	35.3	33.2	30.8	28.8	29.2	27.7	25.1	24.0	21.8	21.2
Consumer credit	18.4	23.6	23.0	22.0	16.2	14.4	15.0	14.9	15.0	12.6	10.5
Other	11.4	11.7	10.2	8.8	12.6	14.8	12.7	10.2	9.0	9.2	10.7
Provision for income taxes	11.2	14.8	15.7	15.0	14.4	14.7	13.4	11.7	10.8	9.4	9.0
Consumer credit	7.4	10.4	11.5	11.2	9.7	9.2	8.9	8.3	7.9	6.5	6.0
Other	3.8	4.4	4.2	3.8	4.7	5.5	4.5	3.4	2.9	2.9	3.0
Net profit	18.6	20.5	17.5	15.8	14.4	14.5	14.3	13.4	13.2	12.4	12.2
Consumer credit	11.0	13.2	11.5	10.7	6.5	5.2	6.2	6.6	7.1	6.0	4.5
Other	7.6	7.3	6.0	5.1	7.9	9.3	8.1	6.8	6.1	6.4	7.7
Dividends	7.4	8.2	7.7	8.8	7.2	7.4	7.7	7.2	6.9	7.3	7.0
Preferred	1.1	1.2	1.2	0.9	0.7	0.6	0.6	1.0	1.1	1.0	1.0
Common	6.3	7.0	6.5	7.9	6.5	6.8	7.1	6.2	5.8	6.3	6.0

Source: See source to Table C-1.

TABLE C-4

COMPONENTS OF GROSS FINANCE CHARGES ON CONSUMER CREDIT AT SALES FINANCE COMPANIES, 1949-59
(dollars per $100 of average outstanding consumer credit)

Item	1949	1950	1951	1952	1953	1954	1955	1956	1957	1958	1959
Gross finance charges[a]	20.04	20.38	19.12	19.94	17.99	17.12	16.53	15.62	16.56	16.95	16.59
Dealer's share of gross finance charges	4.11	4.11	3.76	3.79	3.40	3.10	3.14	2.79	2.96	2.98	2.95
Lender's gross revenue	15.93	16.27	15.36	16.15	14.59	14.02	13.39	12.83	13.60	13.97	13.64
Operating expenses	9.45	8.46	7.56	8.37	8.04	8.03	7.52	6.78	7.03	8.06	7.74
Salaries	4.16	3.93	3.68	3.86	3.57	3.70	3.36	3.12	3.30	3.54	3.47
Occupancy costs	.43	.47	.41	.37	.40	.42	.40	.38	.39	.45	.43
Advertising	.22	.25	.27	.26	.26	.28	.27	.28	.28	.30	.31
Provision for losses	2.01	1.36	1.04	1.57	1.59	1.44	1.39	1.11	1.12	1.68	1.46
Actual losses[b]	(1.16)	(.73)	(.88)	(1.17)	(1.41)	(1.23)	(.83)	(.97)	(.95)	(1.77)	(1.11)
Other	2.63	2.45	2.16	2.31	2.22	2.19	2.10	1.89	1.94	2.09	2.07
Nonoperating expenses	6.48	7.81	7.80	7.78	6.55	5.99	5.87	6.05	6.57	5.91	5.90
Cost of nonequity funds	2.58	2.48	2.68	2.91	3.28	3.15	3.08	3.53	3.95	3.74	4.02
Income taxes	1.59	2.36	2.62	2.52	1.97	1.82	1.63	1.40	1.38	1.16	1.07
Cost of equity funds (lender's profit)	2.31	2.97	2.50	2.35	1.30	1.02	1.16	1.12	1.24	1.01	.81
Dividends	.97	1.09	1.00	1.16	.47	.42	.70	.57	.61	.59	.48
Retained	1.34	1.88	1.50	1.19	.83	.60	.46	.55	.63	.42	.33

Source: See source to Table C-1.

[a]Includes all finance charges and fees collected on consumer credit activities. Charges for insurance are not included and the cost of free insurance provided to borrowers was deducted.

[b]Net of recoveries.

TABLE C-5

SELECTED RATIOS FOR SALES FINANCE COMPANIES, 1949-59
(per cent)

	1949	1950	1951	1952	1953	1954	1955	1956	1957	1958	1959
Ratios to total assets of:											
Earnings	15.7	16.4	15.6	15.9	15.1	14.9	14.1	13.2	13.5	13.1	13.4
Operating expenses	9.3	8.8	8.4	8.6	8.0	7.9	7.5	6.8	6.9	7.0	7.1
Net operating income	6.4	7.6	7.2	7.3	7.1	7.0	6.6	6.4	6.6	6.1	6.3
Cost of funds	2.1	2.1	2.3	2.5	2.9	2.8	2.8	3.2	3.4	3.3	3.5
Net profit before taxes	4.3	5.5	5.0	4.8	4.2	4.2	3.8	3.2	3.2	2.8	2.8
Provision for income taxes	1.6	2.3	2.4	2.4	2.1	2.1	1.8	1.5	1.4	1.2	1.2
Net profits	2.7	3.2	2.6	2.4	2.1	2.1	2.0	1.7	1.8	1.6	1.6
Ratios to equity funds of:											
Net profits before taxes	23.6	30.6	27.9	28.1	26.9	27.3	25.7	22.7	21.7	18.7	17.9
Net profits	14.7	17.6	14.4	14.1	13.4	13.5	13.2	12.1	11.9	10.5	10.3
Dividends	5.8	7.3	6.7	7.8	6.7	6.8	6.8	6.7	6.2	6.3	5.9
Ratios of earnings to earning assets:											
Total earnings	18.2	18.6	17.4	18.0	17.3	16.7	15.6	14.2	14.8	15.2	14.7
Consumer credit earnings	15.9	16.3	15.4	16.2	14.6	14.0	13.4	12.8	13.6	14.0	13.6
Automobile paper[a]	15.5	15.5	14.3	14.7	13.2	12.1	11.4	10.9	11.9	12.0	11.7
Personal loans	25.0	23.7	23.3	24.1	23.5	23.3	24.1	22.0	22.1	21.3	21.5
Ratios of gross finance charges to consumer receivables for:											
All types of consumer credit	20.0	20.4	19.1	19.9	18.0	17.1	16.5	15.6	16.6	17.0	16.6
Automobile paper	20.4	20.4	18.9	19.4	17.5	16.0	15.0	14.3	15.7	16.0	15.8
Personal loans	25.0	23.7	23.3	24.1	23.5	23.3	24.1	22.0	22.1	21.3	21.5
Ratios of cost of nonequity funds to:											
Total debt	3.0	3.0	3.3	3.5	3.9	3.7	3.6	4.1	4.5	4.3	4.5
Total nonequity funds	2.6	2.6	2.9	3.1	3.4	3.3	3.3	3.7	4.1	3.9	4.2

Source: See source to Table C-1.

a Excludes dealer participation.

Supplementary Tabulations for Commercial Banks

TABLE D-1

DISTRIBUTION OF SOURCES AND USES OF FUNDS OF COMMERCIAL BANKS,
END OF YEAR, 1954-59
(per cent)

Item	1954	1955	1956	1957	1958	1959
Sources of funds:						
Debt, total	--	.1	.1	--	--	--
Deposits, total	90.2	90.1	89.6	89.4	89.3	89.0
Demand	65.5	65.0	64.4	63.6	62.4	61.8
Time	24.7	25.1	25.2	25.8	26.9	27.2
Dealer reserves	.3	.1	.2	.2	.1	.2
Other liabilities	1.1	1.0	1.0	1.0	1.0	.9
Total nonequity funds	91.6	91.3	90.9	90.6	90.4	90.1
Equity funds, total	8.4	8.7	9.1	9.4	9.6	9.9
Reserves	1.2	1.3	1.4	1.5	1.6	1.9
Stock and surplus	7.2	7.4	7.7	7.9	8.0	8.0
Total	100.0	100.0	100.0	100.0	100.0	100.0
Uses of funds:						
Earning assets, gross	76.5	74.7	74.1	74.1	75.5	74.6
Consumer credit	5.0	6.2	6.6	6.0	5.5	6.3
Other	71.5	68.5	67.5	68.1	70.0	68.3
<u>less</u>						
Unearned income (consumer)	.2	.5	.5	.7	.5	.6
Earning assets, net	76.3	74.2	73.6	73.4	75.0	74.0
Consumer credit	4.8	5.9	6.1	5.3	5.0	5.7
Automobile paper, direct	1.3	1.6	1.6	1.4	1.2	1.4
Automobile paper, indirect	1.2	1.5	1.7	1.4	1.2	1.4
Other goods paper	.6	.8	.8	.6	.6	.4
Modernization loans	.9	.9	.9	.8	.8	.9
Personal loans	.8	1.1	1.1	1.1	1.2	1.6
Other	71.5	68.3	67.5	68.1	70.0	68.3
Cash and bank balances	22.5	24.6	25.1	25.2	23.6	24.5
Other assets	1.2	1.2	1.3	1.4	1.4	1.5
Total	100.0	100.0	100.0	100.0	100.0	100.0

Source: All data are averages of ratios for nine sample banks unless noted.
See Appendix A for a description of the sample and of the processing of the data.
Detail may not add to the totals because of rounding.

144

TABLE D-2

DISTRIBUTION OF SOURCES AND USES OF FUNDS OF COMMERCIAL BANKS,
AVERAGES OF BEGINNING AND END OF YEAR, 1955-59
(per cent)

Item	1955	1956	1957	1958	1959
Sources of funds:					
Debt, total	--	.1	--	--	.1
Deposits, total	90.2	89.9	89.5	89.3	89.0
Demand	73.7	73.5	72.9	72.0	72.2
Time	16.5	16.4	16.6	17.3	16.8
Dealer reserves	.2	.2	.2	.2	.2
Other liabilities	1.0	1.0	1.0	1.0	1.0
Total nonequity funds	91.4	91.1	90.7	90.5	90.2
Equity funds, total	8.6	8.9	9.3	9.5	9.8
Reserves	1.3	1.3	1.5	1.6	1.6
Stock and surplus	7.3	7.6	7.8	7.9	8.2
Total	100.0	100.0	100.0	100.0	100.0
Uses of funds:					
Earning assets, gross	78.0	77.0	76.8	77.8	77.6
Consumer credit	5.8	7.3	6.7	6.3	6.3
Other	72.2	69.7	70.1	71.5	71.3
less					
Unearned income (consumer)	.4	.6	.5	.4	.5
Earning assets, net	77.6	76.4	76.3	77.4	77.1
Consumer credit	5.3	6.7	6.2	5.9	5.8
Automobile paper, direct	2.3	2.8	2.4	2.1	2.2
Automobile paper, indirect	.8	1.2	1.2	1.1	1.3
Other goods paper	.6	.7	.7	.7	.2
Modernization loans	.7	.8	.7	.7	.6
Personal loans	.9	1.2	1.2	1.3	1.5
Other	72.3	69.7	70.1	71.5	71.3
Cash and bank balances	21.2	22.1	22.2	21.1	21.3
Other assets	1.2	1.5	1.5	1.5	1.6
Total	100.0	100.0	100.0	100.0	100.0

Source: See source to Table D-1.

TABLE D-3

DISTRIBUTION OF EARNINGS AND EXPENSES OF COMMERCIAL BANKS, 1955-59
(per cent)

Item	1955	1956	1957	1958	1959
Earnings	100.0	100.0	100.0	100.0	100.0
Consumer credit	14.3	14.4	13.4	12.7	12.7
Other	85.7	85.6	86.6	87.3	87.3
Operating expenses	38.0	38.2	34.5	29.7	43.8
Consumer credit	6.2	6.2	5.6	5.4	6.2
Other	31.8	32.0	28.9	24.3	37.6
Net operating income	62.0	61.8	65.5	70.3	56.2
Consumer credit	8.1	8.2	7.8	7.3	6.5
Other	53.9	53.6	57.7	63.0	49.7
Cost of funds	28.7	27.7	29.1	30.0	25.1
Consumer credit	2.2	2.4	2.3	2.2	1.9
Other	26.5	25.3	26.8	27.8	23.2
Net profit before taxes	33.3	34.1	36.4	40.3	31.1
Consumer credit	5.9	5.9	5.5	5.1	4.6
Other	27.4	28.2	30.9	35.2	26.5
Provision for income taxes	15.6	15.9	18.0	19.7	14.3
Consumer credit	1.8	1.8	2.0	1.7	1.3
Other	13.8	14.1	16.0	18.0	13.0
Net profit	17.7	18.2	18.4	20.6	16.8
Consumer credit	4.0	4.0	3.5	3.4	3.3
Other	13.7	14.2	14.9	17.2	13.5
Dividends	9.8	10.6	9.5	10.0	11.1

Source: See source to Table D-1.

TABLE D-4

COMPONENTS OF GROSS FINANCE CHARGES ON CONSUMER CREDIT
AT COMMERCIAL BANKS, 1955-59
(dollars per $100 of average outstanding consumer credit)

Item	1955	1956	1957	1958	1959
Gross finance charges[a]	8.62	9.16	9.43	9.47	10.04
Dealer's share of gross finance charges	.40	.44	.48	.48	.62
Lender's gross revenue	8.22	8.72	8.95	8.99	9.42
Operating expenses	3.76	3.86	3.96	4.14	4.17
Salaries	2.11	2.23	2.33	2.38	2.33
Occupancy costs	.22	.21	.22	.23	.23
Advertising	.24	.24	.23	.30	.34
Provision for losses	.31	.28	.31	.28	.28
Actual losses	(.13)	(.28)	(.33)	(.17)	(.15)
Other	.88	.90	.87	.95	.99
Nonoperating expenses	4.46	4.86	4.99	4.85	5.25
Cost of nonequity funds	1.16	1.28	1.46	1.47	1.50
Income taxes	1.13	1.28	1.39	1.32	1.33
Cost of equity funds (lender's profit)	2.17	2.30	2.14	2.06	2.42
Dividends	1.31	1.44	1.20	1.05	1.49
Retained	.86	.86	.94	1.01	.93

Source: See source to Table D-1.
a
Includes all finance charges and fees collected on consumer credit activities. Charges for insurance are not included and the cost of free insurance provided to borrowers was deducted.

147

TABLE D-5

SELECTED RATIOS FOR COMMERCIAL BANKS, 1955-59
(per cent)

	1955	1956	1957	1958	1959
Ratios to total assets of:					
Earnings	3.0	3.4	3.7	3.6	3.9
Operating expenses	1.2	1.3	1.3	1.2	1.4
Net operating income	1.9	2.1	2.4	2.5	2.5
Cost of funds	.9	1.0	1.1	1.1	1.1
Net profit before taxes	1.0	1.2	1.3	1.4	1.4
Provisions for income taxes	.5	.5	.7	.7	.6
Net profits	.5	.6	.7	.7	.7
Ratios to equity funds of:					
Net profits before taxes	12.5	13.6	14.8	15.5	14.5
Net profits	6.5	7.1	7.4	7.9	7.6
Dividends	3.7	4.2	3.9	3.9	4.5
Ratios of earnings to earning assets					
Total earnings	4.0	4.5	5.0	4.9	5.3
Consumer credit earnings, total[a]	8.2	8.7	9.0	9.0	9.4
Automobile paper, direct[a]	10.4	9.3	9.3	8.8	8.8
Automobile paper, indirect[ab]	7.8	7.6	7.8	7.6	7.6
Other goods paper[a]	10.0	10.5	11.0	10.6	11.2
Modernization loans[a]	6.6	7.7	7.8	8.0	9.0
Personal loans[a]	9.5	10.4	10.4	10.2	10.9
Ratios of cost of nonequity funds to:					
Total debt and deposits	1.0	1.1	1.2	1.2	1.3
Total nonequity funds	.9	1.0	1.2	1.2	1.2
Ratio of interest on time deposits to time deposits	1.2	1.6	2.1	2.4	2.7

Source: See source to Table D-1.

[a]Based on a sample of eight banks not all of which were included in the tabulations that provided other ratios.

[b]Excludes dealer participation.

Supplementary Tabulations for Federal Credit Unions

TABLE E-1

DISTRIBUTION OF SOURCES AND USES OF FUNDS OF FEDERAL CREDIT UNIONS,
END OF YEAR, 1949-59
(per cent)

Item	1948	1949	1950	1951	1952	1953	1954	1955	1956	1957	1958	1959
Sources of funds:												
Debt	2.3	2.8	3.3	1.7	2.4	2.5	1.9	2.3	2.3	2.3	1.8	2.5
Other liabilities	.3	.2	.2	.3	.3	.3	.3	.3	.2	.3	.4	.5
Total nonequity funds	2.6	3.0	3.5	2.0	2.7	2.8	2.2	2.6	2.5	2.6	2.2	3.0
Equity funds, total	97.4	97.0	96.5	98.0	97.3	97.2	97.8	97.4	97.5	97.4	97.8	97.0
Shares	90.9	90.1	89.2	90.6	90.2	89.9	90.1	89.6	89.3	88.8	89.0	88.2
Reserves and surplus	6.5	6.9	7.3	7.4	7.1	7.3	7.7	7.8	8.2	8.6	8.8	8.8
Total	100.0	100.0	100.0	100.0	100.0	100.0	100.0	100.0	100.0	100.0	100.0	100.0
Uses of funds:												
Earning assets, net	87.9	89.2	89.1	86.7	89.2	90.4	89.8	91.0	91.4	91.6	91.3	93.1
Consumer credit	53.3	58.9	65.0	59.4	62.7	67.2	66.0	68.1	68.6	70.3	67.8	70.8
Other	34.6	30.3	24.1	27.3	26.6	23.2	23.8	22.9	22.8	21.3	23.5	22.3
Cash and bank balances	11.7	10.3	10.4	12.6	10.0	9.0	9.5	8.3	7.8	7.6	7.6	5.9
Other assets	.4	.5	.5	.7	.7	.6	.7	.7	.8	.8	1.1	1.0
Total	100.0	100.0	100.0	100.0	100.0	100.0	100.0	100.0	100.0	100.0	100.0	100.0

Source: Ratios were computed from data for all federal credit unions published by the Bureau of Federal Credit Unions. See Appendix A for a description of the processing of the data. Detail may not add to totals because of rounding.

TABLE E-2

DISTRIBUTION OF SOURCES AND USES OF FUNDS OF FEDERAL CREDIT UNIONS,
AVERAGE OF BEGINNING AND END OF YEAR, 1949-59
(per cent)

Item	1949	1950	1951	1952	1953	1954	1955	1956	1957	1958	1959
Sources of funds:											
Debt	2.6	3.1	2.4	2.1	2.5	2.2	2.1	2.3	2.3	2.1	2.2
Other liabilities	.3	.2	.2	.3	.3	.3	.3	.3	.3	.3	.4
Total nonequity funds	2.9	3.3	2.6	2.4	2.8	2.5	2.4	2.6	2.6	2.4	2.6
Equity funds, total	97.1	96.7	97.4	97.6	97.2	97.5	97.6	97.4	97.4	97.6	97.4
Shares	90.5	89.6	90.0	90.3	89.9	90.0	89.8	89.4	89.1	88.9	88.6
Reserves and surplus	6.6	7.1	7.4	7.3	7.3	7.5	7.8	8.0	8.3	8.7	8.8
Total	100.0	100.0	100.0	100.0	100.0	100.0	100.0	100.0	100.0	100.0	100.0
Uses of funds:											
Earning assets, net	88.6	89.1	87.7	88.1	89.8	90.1	90.5	91.2	91.5	91.5	92.2
Consumer credit	56.3	62.3	61.9	61.2	65.2	66.6	67.2	68.4	69.5	69.0	69.4
Other	32.3	26.8	25.8	26.9	24.6	23.5	23.3	22.8	22.0	22.5	22.8
Cash and bank balances	10.9	10.3	11.6	11.1	9.4	9.2	8.8	8.0	7.7	7.6	6.7
Other assets	.5	.6	.7	.8	.8	.7	.7	.8	.8	.9	1.1
Total	100.0	100.0	100.0	100.0	100.0	100.0	100.0	100.0	100.0	100.0	100.0

Source: See source to Table E-1.

TABLE E-3

DISTRIBUTION OF EARNINGS AND EXPENSES OF FEDERAL CREDIT UNIONS, 1949-59

Item	1949	1950	1951	1952	1953	1954	1955	1956	1957	1958	1959
Earnings	100.0	100.00	100.0	100.0	100.0	100.0	100.0	100.0	100.0	100.0	100.0
Consumer credit[a]	85.2	88.7	89.5	87.9	89.3	89.7	89.9	89.9	89.4	88.9	88.0
Other	14.8	11.3	10.5	12.1	10.7	10.3	10.1	10.1	10.6	11.1	12.0
Operating expenses[b]	31.6	30.0	32.4	31.3	30.1	33.0	28.7	30.5	30.8	32.2	31.8
Consumer credit	31.6	30.0	32.4	31.3	30.1	33.0	28.7	30.5	30.8	32.2	31.8
Other[c]	--	--	--	--	--	--	--	--	--	--	--
Net operating income	68.4	70.0	67.6	68.7	69.9	67.0	71.3	69.5	69.2	67.8	68.2
Consumer credit	53.6	58.7	57.1	56.6	59.2	56.7	61.2	59.4	58.6	56.7	56.2
Other	14.8	11.3	10.5	12.1	10.7	10.3	10.1	10.1	10.6	11.1	12.0
Cost of funds[d]	1.0	1.4	1.1	1.0	1.2	1.0	1.1	1.1	1.3	1.1	1.1
Consumer credit	.6	1.0	.8	.7	.9	.7	.8	.8	1.0	.8	.8
Other	.4	.4	.3	.3	.3	.3	.3	.3	.3	.3	.3
Net income[e]	67.4	68.6	66.5	67.7	68.7	66.0	70.2	68.4	67.9	66.7	67.1
Consumer credit	53.0	57.7	56.3	55.9	58.3	56.0	60.4	58.6	57.6	55.9	55.4
Other	14.4	10.9	10.2	11.8	10.4	10.0	9.8	9.8	10.3	10.8	11.7
Dividends	42.3	41.1	41.6	42.9	42.2	42.5	42.8	44.4	44.9	46.2	46.4

Source: See source to Table E-1.

[a] Interest on loans minus cost of free life insurance for borrowers and minus interest refunds.

[b] Excludes cost of borrowers' and savers' life insurance, interest costs, and estimate of cost of handling share accounts. Includes losses charged off on loans.

[c] No expenses were allocated to investment in nonconsumer assets as costs of placing funds in U.S. government securities and savings loan shares are relatively small and could not be segregated.

NOTES TO TABLE E-3 (concluded)

d
Cost of funds was distributed between consumer and nonconsumer on the basis of the percentage distribution of average earning assets for year.
e
Residual after operating expenses and cost of funds. Includes two items not usually included in profits of private institutions: cost of handling share accounts and free life insurance for shareholders.

TABLE E-4

COMPONENTS OF GROSS FINANCE CHARGES ON CONSUMER CREDIT AT FEDERAL CREDIT UNIONS, 1949-59
(dollars per $100 of average outstanding consumer credit)

Item	1949	1950	1951	1952	1953	1954	1955	1956	1957	1958	1959
Unadjusted finance charges	9.86	10.25	10.10	10.02	10.22	10.10	10.10	10.05	10.17	10.08	10.04
Adjusted gross finance charges [a] (lender's gross revenue)	9.40	9.73	9.63	9.51	9.67	9.55	9.62	9.52	9.33	9.21	9.13
Operating expenses	3.48	3.28	3.49	3.39	3.26	3.52	3.07	3.23	3.21	3.34	3.30
Salaries	2.10	1.93	2.05	2.06	1.90	1.85	1.82	1.80	1.80	1.79	1.77
Occupancy costs [b]								.06	.06	.06	.06
Advertising [b]								.08	.07	.07	.07
Losses charged off	.30	.27	.32	.23	.25	.56	.12	.31	.30	.41	.38
Other [c]	1.08	1.08	1.12	1.10	1.11	1.11	1.13	.98	.98	1.01	1.02
Nonoperating expenses	5.92	6.45	6.14	6.12	6.41	6.03	6.55	6.29	6.12	5.87	5.83
Cost of nonequity funds	.11	.15	.12	.11	.13	.11	.12	.12	.13	.11	.12
Cost of equity funds	5.81	6.30	6.02	6.01	6.28	5.92	6.43	6.17	5.99	5.76	5.71
Dividends	3.77	3.88	3.84	3.91	3.93	3.89	3.99	4.07	4.01	4.04	4.00
Retained	1.49	1.90	1.47	1.41	1.67	1.35	1.75	1.40	1.27	.98	.98
Services to shareholders [d]	.55	.52	.71	.69	.68	.68	.69	.70	.71	.74	.73

Source: See source to Table E-1.

[a] Includes all finance charges and fees collected on consumer credit activities. The cost of free insurance provided borrowers and interest refunds were deducted.

[b] Separate figures are not available prior to 1955.

[c] Includes occupancy and advertising costs prior to 1956.

[d] Includes cost of free life insurance for shareholders from 1952 to 1959 and estimates of cost of handling share accounts for entire period.

TABLE E-5

SELECTED RATIOS FOR FEDERAL CREDIT UNIONS, 1949-59

(per cent)

	1949	1950	1951	1952	1953	1954	1955	1956	1957	1958	1959
Ratios to total assets of:											
Earnings[a]	6.2	6.8	6.7	6.6	7.1	7.1	7.2	7.3	7.3	7.2	7.2
Operating expenses	2.0	2.1	2.2	2.1	2.1	2.3	2.1	2.2	2.2	2.3	2.3
Net operating income	4.3	4.8	4.5	4.6	4.9	4.7	5.1	5.0	5.0	4.8	4.9
Cost of funds	.1	.1	.1	.1	.1	.1	.1	.1	.1	.1	.1
Net profits[b]	4.2	4.7	4.4	4.5	4.9	4.7	5.0	5.0	4.9	4.8	4.8
Ratios to equity funds of:											
Net income[b]	4.3	4.9	4.6	4.6	5.0	4.8	5.2	5.1	5.1	4.9	5.0
Dividends	2.7	2.9	2.9	2.9	3.1	3.1	3.2	3.3	3.3	3.4	3.4
Ratios of earnings to earning assets:											
Total earnings[a]	7.0	7.7	7.6	7.5	7.9	7.9	7.9	8.0	7.9	7.8	7.8
Consumer credit earnings[a]	9.4	9.7	9.6	9.5	9.7	9.6	9.6	9.5	9.3	9.2	9.1
Other earnings	2.9	2.9	2.7	3.0	3.1	3.1	3.1	3.2	3.5	3.5	3.8
Ratios of cost of nonequity funds to:											
Total debt	2.4	3.1	3.1	3.2	3.5	3.3	3.7	3.6	4.0	3.8	3.8
Total nonequity funds	2.2	2.9	2.8	2.9	3.1	3.0	3.2	3.2	3.6	3.3	3.1

Source: See source to Table E-1.

a
Excludes interest refunds and cost of free insurance provided borrowers.

b
Includes cost of insurance provided shareholders and estimate of cost of handling share accounts.

INDEX

157